# Shaman Pathways

# Black Horse, White Horse

## Power Animals Within Traditional Witchcraft

Shaman Pathways

# Black Horse, White Horse

Power Animals Within
Traditional Witchcraft

Mélusine Draco

MOON
BOOKS

Winchester, UK
Washington, USA

First published by Moon Books, 2013
Moon Books is an imprint of John Hunt Publishing Ltd., Laurel House, Station Approach,
Alresford, Hants, SO24 9JH, UK
office1@jhpbooks.net
www.johnhuntpublishing.com
www.moon-books.net

For distributor details and how to order please visit the 'Ordering' section on our website.

Text copyright: Mélusine Draco 2012

ISBN: 978 1 78099 747 6

A CIP catalogue record for this book is available from the British Library.

Design and cover photograph: Stuart Davies

Printed and bound by CPI Group (UK) Ltd, Croydon, CR0 4YY

We operate a distinctive and ethical publishing philosophy in all
areas of our business, from our global network of authors to
production and worldwide distribution.

# CONTENTS

## The Horse

*Here's a toast for all who love*
*Courage, strength and beauty;*
*Whose simple creed is play the game,*
*Ride straight and do your duty.*

*A toast to him who never failed*
*In wagon, cart or limber;*
*Whose gallant spirit never quailed*
*'Fore line of guns or timber.*

*To him whose heart knows no defeat*
*In hunting field or battle,*
*On classic course, at jungle meet,*
*Or turning maddened cattle.*

*A toast to him who'll always share,*
*Your pleasures, wars and labour;*
*The 'view halloa' or trumpet's blare,*
*Lance, polo stick, or sabre.*

*So lift your glass and honour him –*
*Man's staunchest friend and treasure,*
*As true as steel, as kind as love,*
*In action or at leisure.*

*He lives in memories dear and far,*
*Of noble deeds in peace and war,*
*He paid the price for what we are –*
*GENTLEMEN – THE HORSE!*
Colonel Reginald S. Timms
[*Modern Horse Management*, Cassell 1915]

Chapter One

# The Dawn of History

*There is a wonderful sympathy and freemasonry among horsey men.*
*Be one of them, and you will know all there is to know.*
Sir Arthur Conan Doyle, The Complete Illustrated Sherlock
Holmes

In shamanic terms, everyone is believed to have power animals –
guardians that empathise with us, guide us on the spiritual path,
and protect us from harm. Each power animal increases our
inner power by giving access to the wisdom of its kind, so that
negative energy cannot influence our thoughts and actions. A
horse guardian will impart 'horse sense', and endow us with
some of the attributes of a horse; a dog guardian will give 'dog
sense', and bestow some of the instincts of a dog. The animal
kingdom has a wealth of **knowledge** to offer and our animal
guardian communicates this **wisdom** by drawing our attention
to happenings around us ... and repetition of such 'happenings'
is their means of communication that will, eventually lead to
**understanding**.

To fully understand this communication, we need to understand the horse and its relationship with man throughout
history. All modern breeds *(equus caballus)* are descendents of
wild horses that once lived in Europe and Asia and from this one
species, various breeds have been developed over the centuries.
According to the *Encyclopaedia Britannica*, the horse preceded
man on earth by many ages, although there is very little known
about the early development of the animal. 'Where or when the
species was first domesticated (after having been hunted down
and consumed as food by primitive man), and breeding for

improved types originally began are shrouded in prehistory.'

Research to discover when the first horses became domesticated has been carried out by a team from the McDonald Institute
for Archaeological Research at Cambridge University and Bonn
University. This genetic evidence has enabled the team to look
back thousands of years prior to the first undisputed evidence of
domestication, which dates to the horse and chariot burials on
the Ural Steppes around 2000BC. Genetic analysis of more than
600 horses from 25 breeds, reveals that at least 77 ancestral wild
mares passed on their genes to modern breeds, from the
American Mustang to the Shetland pony.

To discover if today's breeds could be traced back to one
ancestral population, DNA samples were compared with ancient
DNA from horse remains found at Viking burial sites from 2,000
years ago, and 28,000-year-old remains preserved in the Alaskan
permafrost. The results indicated that modern horses fall into at
least 17 distinct genetic groups, with DNA comparisons showing
that northern European animals, found in Scandinavia and
Britain, for example, can be traced back to one ancestral type.

Another distinct group could be traced to Iberia, northern
Africa and America – the latter including the Mustangs
descended from domesticated Spanish horses of the 16th century,
taken by the native Indians, and replacing native horses that had
died out around 10,000 years ago. It is even possible that the
Scandinavian and Iberian types, which possibly date back to the
last Ice Age, show that the horse was not driven to extinction as
had previously been believed. As the forest took over, the
animals moved eastwards into the grasslands of the Steppes of
what is now the Ukraine, Kazakstan and Mongolia.

As interesting as the joint Universities' *Proceedings of the
National Academy of Sciences* report is, it can only conclude that
domestic horses came from at least a dozen different locations;
and forensic archaeology does not reveal the kind of injuries
normally linked with riding, in contemporary human remains.

Although it is possible that horses were domesticated by several ancient peoples, the Steppes still seemed the likeliest place for the team to look for the first attempt. Added to this, the range of horse remains from the area is also consistent with the typical makeup of wild, not domesticated animals. As one of the team concluded: "Archaeological evidence has a long way to go before it provides a direct glimpse of how the first horse was domesticated."

Nevertheless, as John Trotwood Moore observed in his tribute to the horse in the *Encyclopaedia Britannica*: 'Wherever man has left his footprint in the long ascent from barbarism to civilisation we will find the hoof-print of the horse beside it'. Anthropology also shows that all the great early civilisations were the products of horse-owning, horse-breeding and horse-using nations, and that 'those in which the horse was either unknown or in the feral state, remained sunk longest in savagery'. In a nutshell, no great leap of mankind was made without the assistance of 'horse power'.

So consistent was this imagery that the glorified figure of 'the man on horseback' became the universal symbol of power in the universal unconsciousness. The image of the horse was stamped upon coinage, sculptured on temples and even elevated to the human pantheon and worshipped as divine. While animal worship has generally been characteristic of tribal races (with the exception of ancient Egypt), only the horse has been accorded religious reverence in the advanced stages of civilisation; it became the theme of poetry and romance and, next to man himself, the most often portrayed in the fine arts.

War-horses were introduced by the Hyksos into ancient Egypt, where they were used to pull chariots rather than mounted, although battle scenes dating from the New Kingdom occasionally show individual soldiers riding. In the *Illiad*, Homer describes four-in-hand chariots and expert riding, with horsemanship obviously becoming quite an art among the Greeks;

while horse races and chariot racing were introduced into the Olympic Games around 1450BC. Horses played a major role in the expansion of the Roman Empire (although the Romans did not equal the Greeks for horsemanship); helped secure the 13th century conquest of China by the Mongols; and still widely used by the military during the First World War.

In Britain, large numbers of mounted warriors confronted the invading Romans, and history records that these war-horses were extremely powerful. Many were taken back to Rome, where they were highly prized. By King Alfred's time, native British stock had been crossed with imported German 'running-horses'. Following the Norman Conquest, William I imported the best type of cavalry horse and a number of fine stallions were brought over from Spain; while the Crusaders brought new breeds from the East. And according to former cavalryman, Colonel Timms: 'The horse in the past has played a tremendous role in history ... and the national character of England has been largely influenced by pursuits in which the horse has been associated.'

Before the arrival of Christianity, the Celts, Romans, Saxons and Danes revered the animal and 'white horse' sites were considered sacred. Of the hill-figure art that has existed in Britain since prehistoric times, fourteen of the 48 figures visible today are white horses; the most famous being that at Uffington, which is believed to date back some 3,000 years. The white horse was also the standard of the Saxons, and was later impressed on hop-sacks as the ensign of Kent; the rampant white horse being the device of the house of Savoy, also descended from the Saxons. The latest addition is a new image carved into the chalk downland near Folkestone in Kent – whose county symbol is still a white horse.

The White Horse of Uffington overlooks the Vale of White Horse in Berkshire and on a clear day it can be seen for a distance of some 15-20 miles. 17th century antiquarian, John Aubrey made the suggestion that the figure was made on the orders of Hengist, the first Kentish-Saxon king, who bore a white horse on his standard. Other sources claim it marks the victory of Alfred the Great over the Danes, while archaeologists have, at varying times, dated it to the Stone, Early Bronze or Early Iron Age. Whatever its history, there is an old folk-belief that the person who stands on the horse's eye and revolves three times with their own eyes closed, will have their wish granted.

Significantly, Wayland's Smithy lies a mile to the west – and below the White Horse there is a deep coomb, or valley, known as The Manger. Wayland's Smithy is believed to be a long barrow from which the chalk has been removed and generally dated to around 2000BC. When the site was excavated in 1920, several burials were discovered; together with two flat iron rods that were identified as the currency similar to that described by Julius Caesar in *Commentarii De Bello Gallico*.

Tradition has it that a traveller could leave his horse at the site overnight and leave payment on the capstone; on his return he would find the animal shod and the money gone. The 'Weland the Smith' legend also gives the first clue of the importance of the blacksmith within the early Mystery Traditions of the British Isles. The ritual importance and significance of the smith were closely associated with his role as a worker with iron and the 'persistent folk-memory of the magico-religious role within the community once occupied by the smith' (*Man, Myth & Magic*) ...

Another reason for the exalted position of the smiths arose from their often being outsiders, itinerant workmen who spoke a different language, practised different customs, and kept the secrets of their profession to themselves ... Traces of such beliefs embodying the supernatural powers of the smith can be found in traditions where he is healer, charmer, and practitioner of the occult. As possessor of the 'Horseman's Word', a secret charm, he was supposed to have control over even the wildest of horses.

As to be expected from all this history, 'horse power' plays an important part in heraldry, where the animal was taken as a form of totem or clan symbol to support the family or tribal image. According to *The Concise Encyclopaedia of Heraldry*, this adoption of tribal, national and personal badges began in prehistoric times and, as civilisation moved forward, evolved into the practice of embroidering the family insignia on to the personal trappings of a nobleman, including the *caparisons*, or ornamental coverings of a knight's horse. The personal seal of Geoffroi de Chateabriand of Brittany (1217) shows a rider and horse, sporting a beautiful peacock-design. The most common heraldic equine forms are more than likely to be found completely furnished for war, when it is referred to as 'caparisoned'; or else rearing on its hind legs, when it is termed either *effaré* or *forcené*. A 'spancelled' horse has two of its legs fettered by a log of wood.

Among the most famous of heraldic horses is the white horse; probably introduced to these shores by the Angles, since it is an extremely ancient Germanic symbol of warfare and strength, later to be represented on the shield of Westphalia and Hanover. On the arms of Naples it was a black horse that pranced, certainly an appropriate charger for the dashing Prince Murat. Donkeys and mules are also seen quite frequently as heraldic devices.

A 'pegasus' is a winged horse, generally represented as *volant* (flying) and *animé* (with an eye of a different tincture to the body itself). This is the winged steed of Apollo and largely connected with intellectual arts. The pegasus borne as the arms of the Inner Temple is said to be an 'imposition'; one of the badges of the Knights Templar was a horse on which two knights were mounted, in allusion to their vow of poverty. 'Probably,' suggests Guy Cadogan Rothery (*Concise Encyclopedia of Heraldry*), 'unwilling to take such a vow the lawyers transformed the two poor warriors into two wings.' Sir John Jervis (Lord St Vincent), for his victory off Cape St Vincent, was assigned the crest of a pegasus springing from a navel crown, its wings charged with fleur-de-lis.

Centaurs also belong to classic legend, where they found their way from the dark regions beyond the Caucasus, 'those lands where man seemed to form one with his steed'. The centaur has a horse's body, but from the shoulders up has the bust, arms and head of a man. This was an emblem of courage, tempered with wisdom. When a centaur bears a bow and arrows it is blazoned as ' sagittarius' and appears quite early as a heraldic device, possibly adopted as a badge by King Stephen in the 12th century.

Unicorns are believed to have come to Europe from India, although there is a well-known representation to be seen on a Romano-Egyptian papyrus in the British Museum depicting a unicorn losing at draughts to a smirking lion. The enmity of these two is an ancient one, which is surprising since the lion was the symbol of martial valour with the unicorn representing purity. Legends surrounding the horn of the unicorn are numerous, it being regarded as 'a sovereign cure for many dire diseases, a grand antidote against all poison'.

The heraldic conformation of the unicorn gives it the body of a horse, the legs of a stag, the tail of a lion, a fine mane, and a single horn springing from its forehead. It is almost invariably white or silver, but it is usually armed and 'unguled' with gold (its hooves gilded). This is the famous unicorn 'supporter' of the royal arms of Great Britain, brought from Scotland by James I. The unicorn is 'gorged' (having a collar, coronet or wreath about its neck) with a royal crown, with a chain attached and reflexed over its back. This being the origin of the famous nursery rhyme: 'The lion and the unicorn were fighting for the crown ...'

In a less martial arena, the horse has also played an important part in the social and agricultural world, with racing and hunting events providing much of the social entertainment, especially in rural areas. During the reign of Henry VIII, the Boke of Husbandry, penned by Sir A Fitzherbert decreed that:

A good horse should have three qualities of a woman – a broad breast, round hips and a long mane; three of a lion – countenance, courage and fire; three of a bullock – the eye, the nostril and joints; three of a sheep – the nose, gentleness and patience; three of a mule – strength, constancy and foot; three of a deer – head, legs and short hair; three of a wolf – throat, neck and hearing; three of a fox – ear, tail and trot; three of a serpent – memory, sight and turning; and three of a hare or cat – running, walking and suppleness.

In English bloodstock the stallion was highly prized; while amongst the Arabs, mares were rarely parted from their owners. Most British thoroughbred horses have had some of their best points transmitted to them from Arabian blood, a horse known as the Darley Arabian being the ancestor of some of the world's best racing stock. A quarter of a century later, the Godolphin Barb was discovered in France pulling a cart and became the progenitor of the modern thoroughbred. This horse had a cat as a stable companion and when he died in 1753 at the age of 29, the cat pined away and died.

In agriculture there were five distinct breeds adapted for farm work: the Cleveland, a heavy coach horse; the handsome Lincoln, the Suffolk Punch, the Clydesdale and the Irish *Garron*, a small, native mountain horse. This type was originally a work-horse used for ploughing and pulling farm wagons, and one of the traditional scenes of rural England was to see a skilful ploughman managing a pair of well-trained horses in the field.

**For the purposes of identification, these are the distinguishing colours of horses in accordance with the following:**

> ➤ **Bay:** A reddish-brown shade, or nut-colour in varying shades. By 'dark bay' is meant a tinge of colour nearly approaching black, except on the flanks and tip of the nose, where they are mostly a reddish colour. Golden bay, or

light bay, has a yellowish tinge. Dappled bays are named for the markings on the rump, which tend to be spots of a darker shade than the rest of the coat. Bay horses are extremely handsome with the mane, tail and points being black. Because this is the most common colour for horses, there appear to be very few superstitions attached to it.

> **Black:** This colour falls into three distinct shades. Coal-black, which is the darkest of all (once much in demand for pulling funeral coaches, etc., as these were often entire stallions, carrying their crests proudly as part of the Victorian death-cult); an ordinary shade of black and a rusty-black, the coat having a reddish tinge. Because of the association with death, black horses were often deemed to be unlucky although the symbol of a powerful black horse could be seen to represent virility – such as the famous Cavalry Black. In Gaelic the black horse represented the West or invisible wind; while in Indian myth the black horse was the colour of sacrifice. Several well-known demons are supposed to appear riding on a black horse; as is the Knight of Wands in the Tarot

> **Chestnut:** Takes its name from the polished skin of the horse-chestnut, both being of the same colour with various hues ranging from light, to reddish, to almost black. (A sorrel is a pale chestnut with a flaxen mane and tail.) It is said of chestnut horses that they are generally very fast or very slow; and the mares are reputed to be very temperamental.

> **Dun:** There are several shades of dun, some of them being very striking, with a yellowish hue, with manes and tails either black or white. Some dun coloured horses have a black line along the vertebrae and points. Dun colouring reflects sunlight and enables the horse to tolerate the heat better than some other colours.

> **Grey:** The grey coat is made up from a mixture of white,

black and bay. Dapple grey horses are marked with round spots, either of black or some other colour. Almost black at birth, as grey horses advance in age they can become almost pure white. Ghost or mythical horses are invariably white or grey but the luck of the viewer depends on local custom: Faerie horses are always white and the Manx water-horse is pale grey, as is the Scottish Kelpie. A Yorkshire saying runs as follows on sighting a white horse, followed by spitting and keeping the fingers crossed until a dog is seen:

*White horse, white horse, bring me good luck,*
*Good luck to you, good luck to me,*
*Good luck to every white horse I see.*

➢ **Roan:** These horses are of a bay, sorrel or dark colour with spots of grey or white thickly interspersed; a mixed colour having a decided shade of red is a strawberry roan. A blue roan has a black coat flecked with white hairs.

➢ **Piebald:** A distinctive black and white colouring that gives rise to a variety of customs involving spitting and crossing the fingers. Many of the 'paint' ponies of the native Americans have these attractive markings and were highly prized amongst the Plains Indians.

➢ **Skewbald:** A distinctive brown and white colouring, although sight of such a horse is more often than not considered unlucky – probably dating from Victorian times and associated with gypsies and their supposed magical powers. For the Welsh, a stray two-coloured horse whinnying near a stable brought disease or death to the horses.

## The Pegasus Ritual (Autumn)

After the autumn equinox, the Square of Pegasus, the great

'landmark of autumn', appears high in the southern sky. This constellation is made up of four easily discernible bright stars: Alpheratz, Markab, Scheat and Algenib and should not be missed as a time to perform a magical working using the winged, white horse. This is the symbol for ambition and so the image should be used to represent a change of life-style or direction, particularly if connected with the intellectual arts.

Spend some time meditating on the direction you wish your plans to take and make sure that everything is clearly set out in your mind. If necessary, write them down on a piece of clean paper in the form of a talisman, but remember to be careful about what you wish for – you may just get it!

Obtain two wing-feathers and several strands of horsehair. Wing, or primary flight feathers are long and pointed, with each having a stiffening shaft nearer to the top than that found in tail feathers. White goose feathers are ideal but if these are impossible to obtain, use whatever comes to hand, but do try to obtain the feathers and hair well in advance of the intended ritual. In preparation, take the horsehair and securely bind the two feathers together to represent your winged ambition. These should be in your sacred space, which should be set out according to your own Path or Tradition but using corn and fresh water for the offerings. Using basic candle magic, take a small white candle and anoint it with a corresponding oil (i.e. for wealth, business, success, etc.), starting at the top of the candle and stroking the oil downwards.

For added focus, place the talisman beneath the candle-holder and use it in directing all your magical energies toward a positive outcome. When you feel you have poured all your energy into making your future plans work, the talisman may then be burned in the candle flame to cement the spell. When the working is over, wrap the bound feathers and ashes in a piece of clean fabric and put them away safely until the spring, when it will be time to 'release' them from their bonds. Close down your

Circle in your normal way.

Ideally, the candle should be allowed to burn itself out naturally, but if this is not possible, snuff out the candle and hold it under cold, running water to disperse the energies. Ideally, dispose of the discarded candle thoughtfully, either by allowing it to burn out in a bowl of water; or by placing it outside. This is why it is better to use small candles or night-lights for spell casting.

Do bear in mind that there are those who simply blow out a candle and then ...

- ❧ either throw it out with the rubbish – in which case their efforts will follow it to the local tip!
- ❧ or put it away to use on another occasion, where conflicting energies will probably neutralise the original spell.

**There are also five important points to bear in mind with this rite:**

- ➢ Do *not* use tail feathers as the aerodynamics are not the same and your ritual may turn base over apex, even running the risk of reversing itself.
- ➢ Try not to be overly ambitious with your plans. Remember when Bellerophon attempted to fly to Olympus on Pegasus, he was punished by Zeus for his presumption, by being thrown from the horse and lamed and blinded as a result.
- ➢ Feathers can be picked up on your daily rambles or obtained from anyone who keeps domestic birds; while horsehair can be found in hedges or obtained from local stables. The difficulty in obtaining any necessary items makes the magical working more potent.
- ➢ The working will take several months to come to fruition and should not be attempted for quick-fix results.

**Warning:** *Magic does not work on its own* and if you want something to succeed, then it will also require some effort on your part. For instance: there's no point in wishing to become a bestselling novelist when you've never written a thing in your life – join a writers' group and set the ball rolling.

## The Pegasus Ritual (Spring)

By the beginning of February (Candlemas/Imbolc), the Square of Pegasus is disappearing in the West and will not return until autumn. This is the time to magically dispose of your empowered wing feathers so that your plans can be given an additional boost. Hopefully, you will have been making some positive moves on the physical plane, while the Pegasus-energy has been working on the astral levels.

Cut the horsehair bindings, so the feathers fall free and choose a time when it is possible to release the feathers into the wind. Drop them from the window of a high building, or leave them in the hedgerow when you're out walking the dog. Take a moment to whisper a message of thanks – and make up your mind to examine *every* opportunity that comes your way. This doesn't mean you have to take up every option ... just give *everything* careful consideration before rejecting it as not being suitable.

It is also extremely important to know what and when to let go. Like all things we cherish, we need to let go and if they wish, they will return – if they don't, they were never ours to begin with. Pegasus will return in the autumn, but hopefully many of the plans you've made together will already be starting to happen and so it will be time to work with him on the next step for the following year – or on something different.

## Equine Correspondences (Classical History)

The horses of King Arthur were (1) **Spumador**, whose name means 'the foaming one' and (2) **Lamri,** a mare, 'the curveter' or 'one who frisks and frolics'. **Symbols: (1) Efflorescent and (2) Friendship.**

**Babiéca:** (Spanish – 'a simpleton'). The Cid's horse survived his master by two and half years, during which time no one was allowed to mount him; and when he died he was buried before the gates of the monastery at Valencia, where two elms were planted to mark the site. The horse was so called because, when Rodrigo in his youth was given the choice of a horse, he bypassed the most esteemed ones and selected a rough colt; whereupon his godfather called the lad *babiéca* (a dolt), and Rodrigo transferred the appellation to his horse. **Symbol: Loyalty.**

**Borak** (Arabian): The mythical 'horse' that conveyed Mahomet from earth to the seventh heaven. It was milk-white, had the wings of an eagle, and had a human face with a horse's cheeks. Every pace she took was equal to the farthest range of human sight. The word is Arabic for 'lightning'. Mahomet's white mule was called **Fadda. Symbol: Sacred.**

**Bucephalos** (Greek): The celebrated charger of Alexander the Great. Alexander was the only person who could mount him, and he always knelt down to take up his master. He was thirty years old at death, and Alexander built a city for his mausoleum, which he called Bucephala. The word means 'ox head'. **Symbol: Comradeship.**

**Carman:** The Chevalier Bayard's horse, given to him by the Duke of Lorrain. It was a Persian horse from Kerman or Carman. Pierre de Terrail was a celebrated French knight (1476-1524) whose name was synonymous with chivalry and fearlessness. **Symbol: Courage.**

**Celer:** The horse of the Roman Emperor, Verus. It was fed on almonds and raisins, covered with royal purple, and stalled in the Imperial Palace. (Latin for 'swift'.) **Symbol: Illusion.**

**Incitatus:** The horse belonging to the Roman Emperor Caligula, made priest and consul. It had an ivory manger, and drank wine out of a golden pail. The word means 'spurred on'.

**Symbol: Unwarranted elevation.**

**Kantaka**: The famous white horse of Prince Gautama of India (Buddha). **Symbol: Purity.**

**Orelia:** The charger of Roderick, last of the Visigoth kings. The horse was noted for its speed and symmetry, but this did not stop Roderick from being routed at the battle of Guadalete on 17th July 711. (Southey took this story for an epic poem in 25 books of blank verse). **Symbol: Swiftness tempered by caution.**

**Shibdiz:** The Persian Bucephalos, fleeter than the wind that was the charger of Chosroes II of Persia. **Symbol: Swiftness.**

**Strymon:** The horse immolated by Xerxes before he invaded Greece. Named from the river Strymon in Thrace, from which vicinity it came. This sacrifice was possibly an attempt to lessen the great losses he expected to suffer during the invasion. **Symbol: Sacrifice**

## Chapter Two

# Magical Perspective

*With flowing tail and flying mane,*
*Wide nostrils, never stretched by pain,*
*Mouths bloodless to the bit or rein,*
*And feet that iron never shod,*
*And flanks unscar'd by spur or rod,*
*A thousand horses – the wild – the free,*
*Like waves that follow o'er the sea,*
*Came quickly thundering on.*
Lord Byron

From a magical perspective, the horse is a symbol of terrestrial or chthonic power, being projected into the heavens and integrated with the sky gods in most of the ancient religions. In classical mythology, Poseidon/Neptune is said to have created the horse and horseracing and, as a result, the animal became sacred to him. It was Gaulish goddess Epona, however, who is recognised as the goddess of horses, asses and mules. Her worship was brought into the British Isles by the Celts, and the *equites singulares*, the foreign imperial bodyguard, introduced her to Rome. The Romans used to place the image of Epona, crowned with flowers on festive occasions, in a small shrine in the centre of the architrave of the stable. In art she is generally depicted seated, with her hand on the head of a horse or ass, or sometimes a dog.

In almost all of the ancient civilisations (with the exception of South America and Egypt), the Sun was believed to be drawn across the sky in his chariot by a team of celestial horses. In this fashion, the Norse god Dag was conveyed through the heavens by the white steed, Skinfaxi, of the 'Shining Mane' spreading light over the whole world. In turn, the Norse moon-goddess, Mani, travelled across the sky in a chariot drawn by Alsvidur, the 'All Swift'.

Diana, goddess of the moon, was also associated with a horse-drawn chariot; as were the gods Helios and Thor; Odin being carried through the clouds on the back of his eight-footed steed, Sleipnir. Many other deities in antiquity, especially in India, were associated with the horse. In Arcadia, Demeter, Greek goddess of fertility in her darker aspect was sometimes shown with the head of a horse. In ancient Greece, an annual horse sacrifice took place at Rhodes where a chariot and four horses were thrown into the sea; while the Spartans made their sacrifice on a mountaintop. 'For thus, whether on the mountains or in the sea, the fresh horses stood ready for the weary god where they would be most welcome, at the end of his day's journey,' wrote Sir James Frazer in *The Golden Bough*. The Egyptian god, Set, was associated with the ass.

In Greek mythology, the hero Hippolytus, a favourite of Artemis/Diana, was killed by being thrown from his chariot and dragged to his death by the horses. Thereafter horses were excluded from her sacred grove because they were held responsible for his demise. According to Frazer, however, Hippolytus, being identified with Virbius, 'the first of the divine Kings of the Wood at Aricia' was possibly a sacrificial vegetation god. On the 15th October in Rome, an annual chariot race took place on the Field of Mars, with the winning horse being sacrificed to guarantee a good harvest for the following year. This was believed to derive from a much older autumn custom that took place on the ruler's cornfields at the end of the harvest.

The horse also played an important part in the harvest celebrations of the British Isles. In parts of Scotland, the last sheaf of the harvest 'the maiden' was carried home and kept by the landowner's wife until the first mare foaled, when it was given as its first food. 'The neglect of this would have untoward effects upon the foal, and disastrous consequences upon farm operations generally for the season [*The Golden Bough*].' In other areas the 'maiden' was fed to a mare in foal on Christmas morning, or to the oldest cow in calf. Elsewhere the sheaf was divided between all the livestock.

This 'corn spirit' is often seen as a horse or mare, and there is a folk-saying that when the corn bends before the wind: 'There runs the Horse'. The corn spirit, in the form of a living mare, was once passed from a farm where the harvest had been cut, to a neighbouring farm where it was still standing. The farmer who was the last to complete his harvesting was therefore obliged to keep and feed the mare all winter. Horses also played their part in the spring need-fire rituals that the early Church denounced as heathen superstition. Of great antiquity even in the Middle Ages, it was still common for the owners of livestock to drive their animals through the flames; a custom lasting until the early19[th] century as a rural practice for preventing cattle-disease and a poor harvest.

Horses played an important part in European fertility rites. By the late 15th century the hobby-horse began to appear in masques and entertainments, having replaced the traditional skull on a pole of earlier times – although its seasonal use differs from region to region. In May Day festivals, the hobby-horse still has a prominent role and turns up wherever they dance the Morris. In Glamorgan and Monmouthshire, the Welsh mid-winter version of the 'hobby' is the *Mari Lwyd*, which appears on Christmas Night; in other parts of the principality the ceremony is associated with the New Year or Twelfth Night. The *Mari Lwyd* was a horse's skull on a pole with a white sheet draped over it, the skull decorated with ribbons and coloured glass to represent the eyes. The man carrying the skull stood underneath the sheet, holding the pole and moving the lower jaw by means of a wooden handle. The party was made up of poets and singers who challenged the local householders to a rhyming contest. Those inside could keep them out so long as they could answer the rhyme, but when they failed, the party could enter and claim food and drink on the house.

The traditional military funeral, where a rider-less horse carries its dead master's boots reversed on either side, behind the coffin, is probably one of the last surviving customs of the important role the horse played in the religious observations of our ancestors. Part of the ancient funerary rites of any important king or nobleman would have necessitated the killing of his favourite horse to accompany him on his journey in Otherworld. As a result, the horse came to be regarded, not only as a spiritual link with Otherworld but also as a kind of psychopomp, which served to conduct the spirit of the deceased on his final journey to join his ancestors.

*Dying for the Gods* and *Roman Britain* chronicle the archaeological findings of horse remains from the early periods of British history. These were either part of the grave goods to accompany a deceased nobleman (or woman); or as some form of sacrificial rite, since many include the remains of a human, horse and dog. At the ancient horse-feasts, chiefs would wallow in a sort of horse-meat stew in order to increase their virility, while some tribes believed horses conveyed messages from the gods, or were the link between this world and the next. Many of these sacrificial customs survived until the 14th century and, as late as the 18th century, horses were still burned alive in a superstitious rite, to dispel disease or as a protective device.

In *The Pattern Under the Plough*, George Ewart Evans offers up the theory that when the horse evolved culturally, there developed a parallel totemic taboo on eating horse-flesh, which has persisted in the British collective unconscious to the present day. The British have a long-standing aversion to eating horsemeat and, at one time, the medieval church issued a clear interdict under Canon Law against breaking the taboo. Despite the modern links to Europe where horsemeat is part of the staple diet, British sensibilities still find the idea of horsemeat offensive.

T. C. Lethbridge in his book, *Witches*, suggested that the name *Iceni* may derive from the old Celtic word *Eachanaidh*, meaning 'people of the horse'. From the eastern part of England, the territory traditionally occupied by the Iceni, the breeding of horses was highly developed throughout historical times. In this area, horses made up plough teams long before other regions changed over from teams of oxen. It is recorded that in Suffolk the horse was harnessed to the plough as early as the beginning of the 12th century – and today, the heart of British horseracing is located at Newmarket.

In Celtic lore, the king, as part of the Rite of Sovereignty, ritually or symbolically mounted a grey mare, which was the embodiment of Epona. Her name is believed to be Gaulish for mare, and it was in this form she was worshipped by the Celtic auxiliary regiments of the Roman army. In this guise, she became the patron of horses, horse-breeding and dogs; who bestowed leadership and prosperity and presided over maternity, healing springs and crops. The Grey Mare is a frequently occurring theme in British folklore with the Grey Mare and her Colts giving their name to a pre-historic site located just down the bridle path from the Kingstone Russel stone circle. The *Mari Lwyd* mentioned earlier, means 'grey mare', suggesting a direct link with the Eponian horse-cult. And as late as the 15th century, the 'King's Grey Mare' was the derogative name given to Elizabeth Woodville, wife of Edward IV: a theme explored by Rosemary Hawley Jarman in her novel of that name.

In the popular Devonshire folk-song, *Widdicombe Fair*, the grey mare is borrowed from Tom Pearce but, having been ill-used by *'Bill Brewer, Jan Stewer, Peter Gurney, Peter Davy, Dan Whiddon, Harry Hawk and old Uncle Tom Cobley … took sick and died.'* For those familiar with the Mysteries, the story is plain but suffice to say that the aforementioned company paid the price for their neglect of the grey mare.

These are the beliefs that have been preserved in country superstitions, folklore and customs, where valid religious observances became debased with the onset of Christianity. But, as George Ewart Evans comments:

> This is the usual course of old discarded images and dogmas: they sink into society's unconscious, the old traditional and unbroken rural culture; or they are kept alive in the games and practices of children who are still inadvertently keeping Epona's memory green by spitting on their finger and wetting the sole of their shoe on those rare occasions when they meet a white or grey horse.

So, from ancient times, 'horse power' has been representative of the turning points of the year: the springtime (fertility/spring equinox) and harvest (death/autumn equinox). For our ancestors, these were the only significant dates in the calendar – the time when livestock was put out to pasture, and the time when it was brought in from the meadows and any surplus killed off to provide winter provisions.

So, perhaps it is not surprising that the horse plays an integral part in our collective unconsciousness, and those who do not show respect for such a sacred animal and its traditions, should never consider themselves pagan, shaman or witch. With the horse playing such an important role in the magical and spiritual lives of our forebears, it is appropriate to include a charm for drawing wealth – and by this we do not necessarily mean *monetary* gain.

## Horse Dung Ritual

Horse dung represents the fertilising agent from which will spring the 'wealth' we are about to request. There is little wrong in petitioning for money to get us out of a hole, but a money charm for great financial gain out of all proportion to our lifestyle can either (a) burn itself out like a damp squib, or (b) backfire if the request is motivated by greed. We each view 'wealth' from differing standpoints and so what we ask for may differ considerably from individual to individual.

Unlike other types of animal dung, that from a horse is easily collected and dried for the purpose of the rite. Obtain a small nugget and keep it in newspaper until it has completely dried out and can be crushed to a powder. Tip as much as is needed into a small jar with a screw-top lid and keep it safe until the appointed hour. In addition you will need several small 'gold' or 'silver' coins to represent the 'wealth' you seek.

According to the planetary attributions, charms for wealth are best worked on a Wednesday under the influence of Mercury, if your request is in terms of abstract wealth, i.e. knowledge, wisdom and understanding. It should be done on a Thursday under the influence of Jupiter if you *are* petitioning for monetary gain. The rite should be performed three hours after sunset according to the methods used by your particular Path or Tradition.

On a large sheet of clean white paper draw a large pentagram enclosed inside a double circle. In between the two circles, draw or write the symbols relevant to your request. This can be as simple or as elaborate as you wish. Place the jar of horse dung in the centre of the pentagram, together with the coins. One by one, drop the coins into the jar with each one representing a single aspect of your request – each having been carefully thought out before the ritual begins. If necessary, write each one down in the form of a script well in advance, so that you can make any appropriate changes *before* finally committing yourself.

**Warnings:**
- Do not ask for more than you are *morally* entitled to.
- Do not expect your request to be handed to you on a plate.
- Do not put in a request to win the lottery!

- ☙ Be prepared to pay something in return.
- ☙ Magical ability is there to be used – not exploited.
- ☙ Greed can quickly manifest into demonic energy if unchecked.
- ☙ Be careful of what you ask for – you may just get it!

Burn the paper in a suitable container and add the ashes to the jar; screw down the top and shake vigorously to mingle the horse dung, coins and ashes. Close down the rite by passing your hands over the jar. Dispose of any leftover dung on the garden as a form of offering. Keep the jar close to hand (in a desk or among your books) and give it a good shake from time to time to re-activate the energy.

## Horse Dung

In case the reader may come to think that the author is joking about the horse dung ritual, it should be noted that this is an accepted ingredient when a continual slow heat is necessary for the alchemical process. To quote Paracelsus: 'Digest in horse dung wine which has been poured in a pelican [still] for two months ... you will see a thin pure substance like a sort of fat which is the spirit of wine spontaneously evolved on the surface ...'

## Equine Correspondences (Classical Myth and Legend)

**Arion** (Greek): Hercules' horse, given to Adrastos. The horse of Neptune brought out of the earth by striking it with his trident; its right feet were those of a human creature, it spoke with a human voice, and ran with incredible swiftness. The word means 'martial', i.e. war-horse. **Symbol: Force or power.**

The horses of Aurora (Greek) **Abraxos** – the letters of this name in Greek make up 365, the number of the days in the year; **Eōos** – 'dawn'; **Phaeton** – 'shining one'. **Symbol: Elemental air.**

**Balios** (Greek – 'swift'): One of the horses given to Peleus by

Neptune and afterwards belonging to Achilles. Like Xanthos, its sire was the West wind, and its dam Swift-foot, the harpy. **Symbol: Changeable**

The horses of Castor and Pollux (Greek): **Cyllaros**, named from Cylla, in Troas, and **Harpagos** – 'one that carried off rapidly'. **Symbol: Impetuosity.**

The horses of Diomedes (Greek): An impetuous, fiery and chivalrous captain of Argos in the Trojan expedition. His horses were **Dinos** – 'dreadful' and **Lampon** – 'the bright one'. **Symbol: Courage**

**Doomstead** (Norse): The horse of the Norns. **Symbol: Fate.**

The horses of Hades/Pluto (Greek/Roman): **Abaster** – 'away from the stars' or 'deprived of the light of day'; **Abatos** – 'inaccessible' and refers to the infernal realm; **A'eton** – 'swift as an eagle'; and **Nonios. Symbol: Elemental earth.**

The horses of Hector (Greek): **Ethon** – 'fiery', **Galathē** – 'cream coloured' and **Podarge** – 'swift-foot'. **Symbol: Heroism**

**Hippocampes:** One of Neptune's horses that had only two legs, the hind quarters being that of a dragon's tail or a fish. **Symbol: Elemental water.**

**Hrimfaxi** (Norse): The horse of Night, from whose bit fall the 'rime-drops' which every night fall as dew on the earth i.e. frost-mane. **Symbol: Renewal**

**Pegasus** (Greek): The winged horse of Apollo and the Muses. Perseus rode him when he rescued Andromeda. Meaning 'born near the *pēge* or source of the ocean'. **Symbol: Ambition.**

**Skinfaxi** (Norse): The steed (1), whose name means 'shining mane', draws the sun-chariot of Dag. While the moon-goddess, Mani, travels across the sky, drawn by **Alsvidur** (2), the 'All Swift'. **Symbol: Sun (1) and Moon (2)**

**Sleipnir** (Norse) Odin's grey horse, which had eight legs and could traverse either land or sea. The horse typifies the wind that blows over land and water from eight principal points. **Symbol: Uncontainable**

The horses of the Sun (Greek): Æthon – 'fiery red'; **Amethea** – 'no loiterer'; **Erythreos** – 'red-producer'. **Lamos** – 'shining like a lamp' and **Phlegon** – 'the burning or blazing one', horses of the noon-day Sun. **Symbol: Elemental fire**

The horses of Sunna (Norse): **Abakur** – 'hot one'; **Alevidur** – 'all scorching'; **Arvakur** – 'splendid'; and **Aslo. Symbol: Searing Heat**

**Xanthos:** One of the horses of Achilles, who announced to the hero his approaching death when unjustly chided by him. Its sire was Zephyros, and dam Podarge. The word means 'chestnut coloured'. **Symbol: Justice**

## Chapter Three

# Superstition

*The Deathless Blacksmith*
*'Tis the Tamer of Iron,*
*The wrestler whose thews*
*Were made for subduing*
*The Thing That Subdues.*
*In splendour of darkness*
*Encaverned he stands,*
*Amid Pow'rs, amid Terrors,*
*The slaves of his hands*
Sir William Watson

Many of the traditional superstitions connected with horses make it very difficult to separate historical fact from fiction. From very early times, horse skulls and bones were among the most frequent finds in old buildings and these were obviously placed there as some form of protection against malevolent forces. A church in Elsdon, Northumberland, has three such skulls in its bell tower, and more than 40 were discovered screwed to the underside of the floor in the Portway public house at Staunton on Wye in Herefordshire. This custom of severing a horse's head for the purpose of acquiring a protective relic, may have given rise to the numerous headless horse legends that abound in the British Isles. It stands to reason that the discovery of horse remains, minus the head, would give rise to all sorts of grisly tales to be told over a pint of ale.

Horse-bones are discovered in the foundations of houses during renovation and these are often removed when the owners discover the macabre remains. Folklore maintains, however, that the bones serve as amulets to keep away the Night Mare. According to one local tradition, if the family owned a good horse and it died, it was the custom to bury the head under the house to retain the virtues of the animal and to protect the building and its occupants from evil. By removing these equine amulets, the new owners may be courting disaster by allowing superstition or squeamishness to interfere with a protection rite. Far better to re-consecrate them and re-inter the remains, rather than tempt providence by getting rid of them. This may be viewed as pure superstition in these days of scepticism, but the disturbance of specially interred remains may invite unwanted psychic phenomena as a result.

The supposed magical influence of horses survives in folklore, such as the placing of horsehair around the throat to cure goitre; or eaten in a sandwich to ward off worms in children – while the pairings from horse's hooves were given to dogs to cure worms. It was also thought that if tail hairs were left in water, they would turn into eels. John Wesley, who had an interest in folk-remedies, recorded that dried and powdered horse 'spurs' (callosities found on the inside of the animal's leg), could be taken as an infusion in warm milk and ale. A cure for whooping cough was to allow a piebald horse to breathe on the patient; consumption or chest complaints could be healed if a sufferer went to the stables and inhaled the breath of any horse there.

Weather lore tells that if a group of horses are seen standing with their backs to a hedge, it is an omen of bad weather. Wispy cirroform clouds have long been known as 'mares' tails' or 'fillies' tails' and are often used to forecast the weather. For example: Mare's tails moving in from the south indicate unsettled weather on the way. This is especially true during the summer half of the year. According to Paul John Goldsack in *Weatherwise* mares' tail cirrus should be considered the weatherman's cloud, for it is covered by thirty-three different points of weather lore that reliably predict future winds, rain or fair skies and perfect summer days.

There are all manner of superstitions connected with the colour of horses. In some areas it is said to be unlucky to dream of a white horse; that black horses are lucky and a piebald is unlucky – in other regions the reverse is true. In certain rural areas it is said to be unlucky to meet a grey (white) horse when setting off on a journey and those encountering one should spit on the ground for good luck. If the horse snorted during a journey this was considered to be a good omen. As we have seen, some people on meeting a white horse will keep their fingers crossed until they see a dog. 'My grandmother made me keep my fingers crossed all the way into town and back again because we happened to see a white horse in a field just after we'd left home and couldn't find a dog anywhere!' remembers one horsewoman.

The markings on a horse are often thought to be an indication of its temperament and ability. A horse with 'white stockings' on the front legs is considered lucky, while an animal with stockings on opposite front and back legs is even luckier. The ideal combination is supposed to be a white star on the forehead and a single white stocking on a hind leg. If the stockings come more than a few inches up the leg, however, it means the horse may be prone to stumbling.

An old country rhyme sums up the beliefs about the white stockings that still hold true for many who may be seen buying horses at auction.

*One, try it;*
*Two, buy it;*
*Three, watch it go,*
*Four, tell 'em 'no!'*

In *Superstitions of the Countryside*, Edwin Radford recorded that the importance of the horse in both battle and in agriculture was 'probably sufficient to account for its pre-eminence in pagan belief and in superstition'. These pagan roots may also account for the associations with witches and the Faere Folk in later folklore. Plaiting a horse's mane and tail with ribbons was originally a method of warding off negative energies – and later became a protection against witchcraft. While in Germany, it was customary to 'free children from witchcraft', by passing them through a horse's collar.

Donald Braider, in *The Life, History and Magic of the Horse*, offers the suggestion that it was during the Middle Ages that the horse began to develop its 'darker' imagery. Early medieval life saw the old pagan ways and the growing Christian belief existing in harmony, but the Black Death changed all that. The church seized the moment and decreed that clinging to all that was evil and sinful in the Old Ways had brought about the dreadful punishment and, as a result, anything that had pagan connotations was pronounced 'devilish'.

The militaristic ruling classes and the rural landowners, however, both of which relied on the horse for their living, retained a healthy respect for the animal. It was the rapidly expanding merchant classes who had scant regard for the horse and looked upon it as a possession, rather than something with which they had a special relationship. Between the church and the middle classes, the horse was ascribed as having supernatural powers closely aligned to witchcraft, for which it was scorned and often maltreated – sentiments that often divide people from different backgrounds, even today.

In her book, *The Witch-Cult in Western Europe*, Margaret Murray refers to the numerous witch-trials that featured accusations of the Devil appearing, either as a horse or mounted on one. Conversely, various saints and holy teachers eventually had equine tales woven about them and eventually folklore was re-written to tell how horses could be protected from witches (or the Faere Folk) who stole them from the stables for riding out.

Needless to say, if we examine British folklore (most of it compiled and published from Victorian sources when it was a popular genre), we find that the 'negative energies' or evil of ancient times has been re-interpreted as witchcraft *per se*. Whenever we see charms or spells to *repel* witches, or protect the wearer from their machinations, we can bet our (riding) boots that originally these were ancient charms to ward off malevolent spirits or bad luck made by witches themselves for protection!

Those who have the ability to interpret folklore and weed out Christian overlay from original folk belief, will begin to see the common thread that runs through the history of horses in Britain. Whenever popular folklore deems that something is evil, ghostly or connected to devils and demons, it usually means that it has an extremely strong link to the pagan past. Genuine Old Craft witches often have some direct, or indirect, connection with the old horse peoples of Europe and would never dream of harming or causing injury to a horse. The rural roots of Old Craft go deep and these sources have been extensively explored by countryman George Ewart Evans, who understood the significance of the horse in the indigenous beliefs of the British Isles.

From an entirely different culture, for those born in the Year of the Horse it will come as no surprise to find that the 'symbolic union between man and horse can either produce a profound, exalting, organic and psychic harmony, or lead to death', according to *Chinese Zodiac Signs.*

The thousand-and-one possible combinations of this subtle game are found in a multitude of traditions, rites, myths, tales, legends and poems: horse of the moon or horse of the sun; white horse or black horse; mount of a hero, on parade and splashed with light; or a phantom horse condemned to wander like a lost soul on the borderline of two worlds, between dream and reality.

For those who have a true and natural empathy with the horse, however, the spiritual symbology of this enigmatic creature transcends mere superstition, for ...

> He is a creature of darkness, emerging from the entrails of the earth or from the depths of the sea. Or, in another sense, he is a black battle-steed carrying on his rump the goddess of shadows, searching for vagabond souls. But in certain traditions the horse also incarnates the spirit of the corn and is the symbol of regeneration. It is he who travels across winter, the country of death and of cold, with the spirit of the sown seed which he transports and protects, replenishing and assuring renewal in the spring.

This 'otherworldliness' has resulted in hundreds of recorded sightings of ghostly horses in folklore, which may in all honesty have their origins firmly in the village inn, rather than actual happenings. Legends of ghosts, Faere Folk and witches have become inextricably entangled in native British folklore and our ancient mythology contains an impressive roll of horses, both spectral and temporal. Horses have long associations with the dead, tending to shy and sweat when troubled by spirits invisible to humans, according to folklorists.

The Celts certainly believed that their souls travelled on horseback to the Otherworld and, according to *Folklore, Myths & Legends of the British Isles*, popular tradition still believes that horses are clairvoyant. 'This power made them vulnerable to enchantment and the forces of evil and, in the Middle Ages [*sic*], witches were said to 'hag-ride' them to their coven meetings, bringing them back to their owners just before dawn, exhausted and drenched in sweat.'

The Victorian death-cult added its own urban myths to the already exhaustive list of superstitions. In the days of the horse-drawn hearse, it was believed to be a fatal sign if the team refused to start with the coffin on board: this meant they would soon be needed again for a member of the same family. Or, if one of the funerary team turned its head and neighed outside a house, it was believed that someone living there would soon die.

*The Realm of Ghosts* by Eric Maple chronicles the many sightings of spectral horses pulling equally spectral coaches across the landscape, including the famous appearance of Sir Francis Drake driving a black hearse pulled by headless horses along the Tavistock to Plymouth road. Although no one can give a plausible reason why he should do so!

The ghost of Dick Turpin can be located riding down Trapps Hill, near Loughton in Essex, and there is even an account of the ghost of a long-dead horse attacking a thief with flailing hooves, in order to protect its former rider.

From Passenham, near historic Stony Stratford, the ghost of Sir 'Bobby' Bannister still rides abroad, having broken his neck in the hunting field and his horse dragging his mangled body home. Since his violent death in 1649, the spirit of the hard-riding lord of the manor has been said to drive his carriage and pair up to the doors of the Manor House on dark and stormy nights, or go for a midnight gallop on his faithful mare.

With all these ghostly goings-on, it is not surprising that much spell-casting concerning horses is to do with protection.

## May Day Protection Rites

Traditionally, birch trees were used for the May Pole, and erected every year for the Roodmass (Beltaine or May Day) celebration. The pole was then kept in the stable yard over the following year to protect the horses from being 'hag-ridden', or having their manes knotted by the Faere Folk.

> ➤ For a more modern version of the tradition, to prevent ill-wishing against a horse and its rider, or any attack by unwanted intruders, fasten a branch of birch hung with red

and white rags or ribbons above the stable door.

> An alternative method of protection would be to make a new besom of birch each year May Day to be kept in the stable yard. The handle of the witches' broom is the male component, while the brush part – made up from birch twigs – is the female.

> A protective talisman can be made by using the 'M' symbol from the runes, which symbolises travel and are therefore appropriate for a horse. Design an appropriate talisman or amulet using this runic device and poke it into the brickwork over the door so that it is completely concealed from prying eyes.

Should there be a report of any cowardly horse attacks being carried out in your vicinity, try the following retribution rite in the form of ...

## The Curse of the Smith

*May their skull be crushed as the iron is crushed by the hammer.*
*May their bowels be torn as the iron is seized by the tongs.*
*May their blood spurt from their veins as the sparks fly from*
*beneath the hammer.*
*May their hearts freeze from cold as the iron is cooled in water.*

This curse is 'thrown' to cast a spell over people who are unknown, and who may be some distance away from the sender. The only equipment you need is a horseshoe nail, which should be bent and twisted with a hammer and pliers, held in the candle flame and plunged into a bowl of water, using the above curse as you do so.

**Any self-respecting witch should be able to handle a tradi-tional curse and this one is particularly appropriate for anyone harming or attempting to harm a horse.**

## Horse Brasses

Until comparatively recent times, horses were believed to be particularly vulnerable to the 'evil eye' and the decorative horse brasses we see today have their originals as amulets to protect the animals. John Vince, writing in *Discovering Horse Brasses*, has to admit, however, that the main difficulty in tracing the use of the 'brasses' as amulets...

> ...is the lack of any supporting documentary evidence, as they came into being long before written history began and, as they were objects tinged with superstition, they never received any attention from early church historians ... But without a long tradition of superstition, how do we explain so many of the ancient symbols on the horse brasses? It is difficult to accept that the Victorian brass designers revived them of their own volition from a past that had not been recorded.

One of the earliest symbols was that of the sun – either with concentric circles or with seven rays or spokes. The crescent, the symbol of the moon is another of the most common charms associated with horses. According to George Ewart Evans, the designs of horse brasses may be divided into two categories: pattern brasses of abstract or geometric design, and figure subjects. The pattern brasses are more likely to have a magical significance, simply because many of the later figure subjects are often commemorative pieces, with little magical significance.

Few brasses were made commercially before 1800 and the old hand-made originals are now extremely rare and should be treasured. Properly cleansed and consecrated, a modern horse brass can serve just as well as an amulet, especially as we are less likely to nail the genuine article to a stable door! Just remember not to haggle over the price if one particular design catches your eye and you require it for magical working.

## Horseshoes

Horseshoes, which came into use about 100BC, made it possible for horses to run on pavement, cobblestones, or over any rough terrain, without splitting their hoofs. The earliest date back to the Romans, who attached the 'shoe' to the horse's foot by cords or leather straps. According to *Old Horseshoes*, the nailed shoe may have originated among the Celts of north-western Europe.

The magical power of a horseshoe derives from the obvious elemental energies that go into its making: the heart of the forge (Fire); the sacred metal, iron (Earth), the cooling (Water) and the bellows (Air) – not forgetting the (Spirit) smith who makes and fits the shoe. Should a cast shoe be found in the road, this should be taken home and nailed above the entrance door – with the prongs pointing upwards – to attract and hold good fortune.

Victorian folklore compilations cite horseshoes as being a protection *against* witches since those collecting the superstitions were unable to differentiate between what magical practitioners would refer to as 'negative energies' and what they saw as evil spirits and witchcraft. This belief was compounded in popular fiction like Sir Walter Scott's novel, *Redgauntlet*, where one character says to another: 'Your wife's a witch, man; you should nail a horseshoe on your chamber door.' While 17th century antiquarian writer John Aubrey, commenting on contemporary social customs, wrote: 'A horseshoe nailed on the threshold of the door is yet in fashion: and nowhere more than in London: it ought to be a Horseshoe that one finds by chance on the Road. The end of it is to prevent the power of Witches, that come into your house.' A popular greeting of the same period expressed the wish, 'That the Horseshoe may never be pul'd from your Threshold.'

Witches themselves were often accused of using horseshoes to further their own ends. In Scotland, Elizabeth Bathcat was indicted because a horseshoe was nailed to the door of her house, and this was seen as 'a devilish means of instruction from the

Devil to make her goods and all her other affairs to prosper and succeed.'

The positioning of the horseshoe also had its significance and it was the smith alone who has the privilege of mounting a horseshoe with the points *downwards*. Any other person using a horseshoe for good luck mounts it points uppermost since according to superstition, it would be at his or her peril to do otherwise. This symbol is confirmed by the 'mark' of the black-smith's trade – the badge of the Worshipful Company of Farriers is a pyramid of three joined horse-shoes each with its points downwards. Another example of the points downwards are those of the city arms of Gloucester, which date back to the 15th century.

## Horseshoe Protection Pouch

From the magical perspective, the only real 'good luck charm' is the horseshoe that has been cast and found by chance. A shoe that has been removed or purchased does not have the same power as one that has been cast whilst riding out, even if it has come from an unknown horse. Sometimes old iron shoes are turned up where land has not been ploughed for many years, and these are worth their weight in gold.

Obviously it isn't possible to decide that we're going out to find a cast shoe – and they are not easily come by. Like all magical tools, however, if the circumstances are right, you *will* acquire your shoe – even if it is given by a friend or an acquaintance, who happened to pick it up without realising the significance. Giving away a horseshoe is to give away luck, so look upon it as an extremely valuable gift. Depending on where you intend keeping the shoe and how you wish to use it, brush off the excess mud and remove any nails. Hang the shoe over door or near the hearth; or alternatively keep it in a pouch and leave the nails in place.

If you wish to use it as a protective piece for your own horse, it is best kept away from prying eyes and curious fingers. Keep clippings of hair from your own horse's mane and/or tail in the pouch and consecrate the whole under the blessings of Epona, with a plea to keep the animal safe and free from harm. Think twice about leaving the pouch in the tack room or stable because others will not be able to resist looking inside. Be prudent and keep it at home, safely hidden away.

## Horseshoe Nails

Most people are familiar with the following rhyme:

> *For want of a nail, the shoe was lost;*
> *For want of a shoe, the rider was lost;*
> *For want of a rider, the message was lost;*
> *For want of a message, the battle was lost;*
> *For want of the battle; the kingdom was lost.*

The humble horseshoe nail has its own significant part to play in Old Craft and is an integral part of the Inner Mysteries. For the beginner, however, it serves as a reminder that if what appears to be the most insignificant part of a magical rite is left undone, this can have serious repercussions later on.

Different types of horseshoe required different types and styles of nail for fixing and the social position of the 'nail-man' was in no way inferior to that of the farrier. To the uninitiated, it might appear that the nail is an insignificant part of the shoeing operation, but it would be the unwise witch who overlooked its importance as an integral element of 'horse power'.

## Horseshoes and Nails

In 1251 Walter le Brun, farrier, in the Strand, London, was to have a piece of land in the parish of St Clements, to place a forge there, for which he was to pay the parish six horseshoes. This rent was paid to the Exchequer every year, and is still rendered to the Exchequer by the Lord Mayor and citizens of London, to whom subsequently the piece of ground was granted.

In the reign of King Edward I, Walter Mares-cullus paid at the *crucem lapideam* six horse-shoes with nails, for a certain building which he held of the king *in capite* opposite the stone cross.

Blount: *Ancient Tenures.*

Taken from Brewers *Dictionary of Phrase & Fable*

## Warning

The horse is still a powerful symbol of rank and position. This means that any magical working using any part of the horse's symbolism, or 'horse power' will draw on a highly volatile energy.

**Principal qualities:** Loyal, enthusiastic, enterprising.

**Principal defects:** Unstable, flares up easily, impatient.

For its size, the horse has a very tiny brain and is as easy to train as it is to frighten. If not controlled the animal will panic at any hint of danger and become dangerous. Some horses can be quick-tempered and react with blind fury, often behaving in an unexpected and unreasonable way. Therefore, the *negative* aspects of the horse, if unleashed magically, can easy run out of control. Any magical working should, therefore, be given meticulous consideration before putting any plan into operation, but the horse's wild and impetuous nature manifests more satisfactorily if the ritual is impromptu and unrehearsed. Spontaneity is the key to equine magic and 'horse power'.

## Equine Correspondences (Folklore)

**The Four Horsemen of the Apocalypse** brought destruction and ruin. The rider of the white horse was armed with a bow, the red with a sword, the black with a balance and on the pale horse rode Death himself. **Symbol: Adversity.**

**Aligero Clavileno:** The 'wooden pin wing-horse' that Don Quixote and his squire mounted to achieve the deliverance of Dolorida and her companions. **Symbol: Dependability.**

**Bayard:** The horse of the four sons of Aymon, which grew larger or smaller as one or more of the sons mounted it. According to tradition, one of the footprints may still be seen in the forest of Soignes, and another on a rock near Dinant. The word means 'bright bay colour'. **Symbol: Community spirit.**

**Dapple:** Sancho Panza's ass (in the *History of Don Quixote de la Mancha* by Cervantes). It is so called because of its colour. **Symbol: Companionship.**

**Kelpie:** The water-horse of fairy mythology. The word means the 'colour of kelp' or seaweed. The kelpie would lure unsuspecting souls to their deaths by encouraging them to climb on its back and then plunging into the water. **Symbol: Deception.**

**Orobas:** One of the seventy-two Spirits of Solomon who appeared in the form of a horse and gave answers to any questions about the past, present or future. **Symbol: Truthfulness.**

## Chapter Four

# The Horse Whisperer

*There's to the horse with four white feet,*
*The chestnut mane and tail,*
*There's to the man that broke him in,*
*His name was Juble Cain*
A version of the Horseman's Toast

In many parts of the British Isles there is still the belief that a single, whispered 'word' will control even the most temperamental of horses. According to horse-lore, this 'Horseman's Word' is a closely guarded secret and only passed from one *true* horseman to another. Needless to say, there are also a lot of conflicting views on what is meant by 'horse whispering'.

In modern parlance it now refers to training by a natural, non-violent method that caught the public's imagination in the book by Monty Roberts, *The Man Who Listens to Horses,* and the Robert Redford film, *The Horse Whisperer*. Roberts, undoubtedly a genuine horseman, demonstrates a method that is a common-sense, practical approach that involves a personal, interaction aimed at winning the horse's trust over a period of time. The secret is to make the horse *want* to co-operate through free-will – not by breaking the spirit – but by studying and learning the language of horses in the wild. This means understanding their psychology and using body language to gain their trust while helping them overcome their fears. Much of this 'new-found' practice comes from America, where horses are traditionally broken by subduing the spirit, unlike traditional British ways where such methods are considered counter-productive.

In rural Britain, however, horse whispering means something

*entirely* different. Right up until the early 1900s there was still an elite class of horse-handlers known as 'whisperers', whose initiates were supposed to exercise their uncanny powers over any horse. This mysterious art enabled the handler to tame the most difficult and obstinate of horses, including the complete paralysis of the animal.

George Ewart Evans in both *The Pattern Under the Plough* and *The Horse in the Furrow,* tells us that in the initiation oath of the Scottish horsemen, only the smith or farrier is mentioned as those other than a true horseman who are entitled to share their lore.

> This was probably no more than a recognition of what became in time an accomplished fact; for the forge and the *travus*, the little annex where the horse is actually shod, were the very stage and spotlight of that horse-control in which most of the skills and secrets of the Horsemen's Society were concentrated.

According to investigations by Evans, these powers were not magical, but due to the use of certain aromatic oils being used to halt or attract the horse. It was from this practice that the horsemen sometimes earned the name *horse-witches*. A reference in Gibbon's *Decline & Fall of the Roman Empire* shows how ancient this practice is. Margaret Murray also records in *The God of the Witches* the case of the horse-witch who was sentenced to the galleys for life because, having felt sorry for the treatment meted out to the postillion horses, cast a spell using vervain 'so that the horses should cease to run'.

Like the rural cunning man or woman, the horseman's skills involve the knowledge and use of herbs and plants to produce the desired effect. This can be dismissed as being non-magical, but there is a tremendous wealth of herbal lore and application needed to produce the substance – in the past that would have been seen as being the possessor of magical, rather than esoteric, knowledge. Some horsemen will admit to certain tricks of the trade that involve the placing of a substance on an object in front of the animal, or on the animal itself, although few will refuse to reveal the ingredients – and quite rightly so!

The real 'trick' is the utilising of the horse's hypersensitive sense of smell for both repelling and calling. There are certain blends of smells that horses find attractive and the experienced horseman (or woman) would place a few drops on his person and stand up-wind from the animals they wish to call. Most of the oils used in calling preparations are aromatic and sweet smelling; repellents are usually concocted from dead animals or urine.

This may often have been the case in many instances of horse whispering tricks, but the interview with former race-horse trainer, Paul Harriss, for *Alphard* magazine reveals that there is more to the true whisperer than mere tricks and wort-lore:

Until the film, *The Horse Whisperer* was released, I hadn't a clue what the term meant – which is rather surprising considering I spent most of my professional years as a racehorse trainer in Newmarket in close proximity to one. The picture of a character with big hobnailed boots, brown cord trousers and a flat cap outlined by Evan John Jones in *The Cauldron* magazine, was an accurate portrait of George Armitage. It would be easy to believe that this taciturn character came from Romany stock although whether he was or not, I really couldn't say.

I first heard about George from my farrier and from certain other trainers in Newmarket; in particular connection with Shergar, the racehorse butchered by the IRA. Shergar was a small horse prone to training problems and it was well-known racing gossip that if George hadn't administered to him beforehand, then it was most certainly to the bookies' advantage. At the time, I owned and ran the public equine swimming pool in Newmarket and was responsible for the swimming programmes to combat un-soundness and training problems in racehorses, also as part of fitness development – hence my connection with Shergar.

The first horse George treated for me, was a large bag of bones called Polar Sunshine, who had failed to live up to his promise as a four-year-old. He was bought and sold several times until someone felt sorry for the walking skeleton, bought him at auction in Ireland, and passed him to me. Despite all the care and attention he failed to respond to treatment and George was called in. Having spent his customary period of time locked away with the horse in its stable, he eventually came out and pronounced that it should remain inside for six weeks and the training programme started from scratch.

From then on there was no holding him and within weeks had turned into a big handsome horse. Three months later he was entered for his first race: a three-mile novice chase, which he won convincingly. He then went on to run in big races at Cheltenham. Unfortunately he developed a leg injury but his owner retired him and after his recovery, used the horse as his own personal hack. No one was ever allowed to go into the stable or box while George 'looked' at a horse. Needless to say, everyone tried to find a chink in the wall, or stood with an ear pressed against the door in an attempt to find out exactly what went on inside. Sometimes it took five minutes, at other times half an hour, but the only thing we ever heard was silence.

With hindsight, I can appreciate that George probably knew all the tricks of the horse-whispering trade and wasn't about to give any of them away. In his defence, and unlike many modern so-call practitioners, he never had a fixed charge for his services. He would be flown down from his home in Northumberland, collected from the airfield by car and ferried to his first yard; each trainer assuming responsibility for getting him to his next call. As far as I know, the routine was to give him an envelope after so many visits. Amounts were never discussed but he was obviously happy with his 'gift' or he wouldn't have continued to call.

He was an extremely modest man, and rarely ventured an opinion unless asked. I can remember one horse being brought to the swimming pool, which looked as though the next stop would be the knackers' yard. The poor animal had taken an hour to get into the horsebox and the owner had brought it to swim in a last ditch attempt at a cure since the vet was ready to put it down. No one in their right mind would have allowed the horse into the pool because we couldn't even get it out of the box!

I heard a familiar voice over my shoulder, 'Can I be of any help?' I'd forgotten George was coming to the yard. The desperate owner agreed to let George have a look and he was duly locked in the horsebox, with both ramps tightly shut. Twenty minutes silence followed until finally George's signal of banging on the side indicated that we could drop the ramp. Upon opening up, George led this previously immovable object tentatively down the ramp; walked the horse in a circle round the horsebox and back up the ramp into the lorry to the total amazement of the owner and myself. The owner was given instructions of what to do with the horse for the next few weeks and the beaming, grateful man was last seen driving off into the distance. How do you explain that? I can't.

There are, of course, dozens of similar stories about George's ability from the length and breadth of the country but no one had any doubts that it was anything other than a genuine gift. As a result, George was treated with a great deal of respect by the Newmarket racing fraternity, and was also a frequent visitor to the stables on the Duke of Norfolk's estate.

Some give the explanation that all this control was exercised through the use of specific oils rather than any inner 'power' and that the horseman's Craft was the 'craft of the trickster ... Magic is the art of creating an illusion that in the end becomes reality'. These views have been endorsed by leading equestrian publications, that have issued warnings of a growing number of fakes claiming to be horse-whispers taking money from gullible owners. As one feature writer rightly pointed out: since no one knew what horse-whispering was, it presented the opportunity for faith healers, psychics and other alternative medical 'experts' to get in on the act.

Paul Harriss continued:

I can state, without a shadow of a doubt that the results George Armitage *regularly* obtained were no illusion. Racing is a billion pound industry and the trainers who called upon his services on a regular basis were seasoned professionals who fully understood the animals they worked with, and had a responsibility to the owners to train a winner. There was no room for the confidence trickster, or the New Age faith healer in that environment, simply because the stakes were high and there was no opportunity for 'wallpapering over the cracks' simply because the sheer power and strength of these horses would quickly expose any quackery.

From what I understood, George was the last of ten generations of Horsemen but his gift was doomed to die with him because he had no son. Personally speaking, I believe that George Armitage possessed one of those old country crafts that do belong to the past and that gave his ability its own special kind of magic. It's sad that those who come after him and lay claim to his Craft, should debase such a man's genuine reputation.

From what modern research suggests, there *was* a secret 'Order' of horse whisperers that had its origins in a horse cult brought into Britain in the Dark Ages by invaders from mainland Europe, or by returning Crusaders. By the late Middle Ages, it had developed as a secret Craft alongside the masons and millers. The Society reached its zenith between the 1830s and 1930s due to the breeding of heavy horses to take over from oxen as a working farm animal and, by 1850, had become a form of trade union, for no farmer could work his fields without an initiated Horseman. According to an article in *The Countryman*, the words of a Scottish folk song echo the training of a young man:

> *Syne I got on for bailie loon,*
> *Syne I got on for third,*
> *And syne of course I had to get,*
> *The Horseman's grippin Word.*

The lyric describes the lad's beginning as a 'loon', or apprentice in charge of the cows; then his promotion to handling the third or spare horse; followed by the finding of an envelope on his pillow on his eighteenth birthday, containing a single horsehair. This was the sign that he'd been accepted to receive the 'Horseman's Word'.

It has also been suggested that the initiation ceremony was a parody of Old Craft rituals of the 16-17th centuries, insofar as the number did not exceed thirteen participants. Certainly the witch-trial reports contain many such similarities, including the shaking of *Auld Chiells's* hand/foot (*Auld Chiells* appears to be a localised name for the Horned God); while certain highly significant elements were incorporated into the rites. For example in this version:

> *Here's to the horse with four white feet,*
> *The chestnut tail and mane*
> *A star on his face and a spot on his breast,*
> *And his master's name was Cain.*

On the following day, the young man was brought into the stableyard at first light and introduced to the farmer as a 'Horseman' who was then entitled to a man's rate of pay. The Horseman's training continued for many years as he was instructed in more and more 'secrets', or tricks of the trade. Firstly he was taught the Four Rules of Horsemanship:

*To Make Him Stand;*
*To Make Him Lie;*
*To Make Him Hip;*
*To Make Him Hie*

The 'secret' taught by the Society was the talking or 'whispering' to the horse that could quieten even the most unruly animal. These techniques would have appeared magical to most onlookers but were, in truth, merely part of the ancient craft of good horsemanship. All experienced Crafters know that resonating sound can produce all manner of effects under particular sets of circumstances and 'whispering' was probably part of this magical knowledge.

Of all the potions used to control horses the most common was the oatcake, which the horseman kept in his armpit overnight. Held beneath the horses' nostrils, the oatcake acted on their sense of smell and made the Horseman's personal body odour familiar to them. The animals would follow the Horseman to the fields, leaving the bewildered owner impressed and wary of the fellow who he accredited with magical powers! Another trick was to plant a pitchfork on top of the muckheap and hitch a team of horses to it. No matter how much they were urged forward, the fork would not move. This was also attributed to the Horseman's magical abilities – which is some ways it was, since by holding a repellent such as toad's blood under the animals' nostrils, the horses would refuse to budge.

One handed-down recipe for oatcake reveals that it contained powdered 'pad' or 'milt' – a fibrous substance removed from a foal's mouth following its birth. Mixed with drawing oils of rosemary, origanum, cinnamon and fennel this blend was first mention by the Roman writer, Pliny, who describes it as a love potion! Similar properties were claimed for hippomane, an outgrowth that colts carry on their heads at birth, which the mother eats. Hippomane was also considered an important aphrodisiac; as a love potion it was sometimes reduced to a powder and mixed with herbs and the blood of the loved one. The lethal combination of horsemanship and confidence has always been a powerful aphrodisiac, and it is not surprising that the local village girls also fell under the spell of the Horse Whisperer! Although a girl who became pregnant by one of these itinerant horsemen apparently didn't share the same stigma as her sister who'd merely gone for a tumble in the hay with a local lad.

The Romany, who first came to Britain in the 15th century, brought a considerable amount of additional horse-lore into Europe. George Ewart Evans maintains that there are no people more skilled in curing (or disguising) a sick horse, and few people know more about horse psychology. Obviously some of the old farm-horsemen learned much of their horse-cult techniques and superstitions from this source. In *The Horse in the Furrow*, Evans also observes that, 'although in the old days the horsemen prepared their own mixtures and got most of their medicines from herbs and trees, as the gypsies do to this day, within the last few generations many have come to use the chemist's shop where many of the substances they needed were to be bought.'

He also quotes a rural chemist as saying: 'They would sometimes have their recipes written down on an old slip of paper, in a half-literate hand … The remedies were traditional, handed down for generations, and some of them had cures the vets had never heard of.' Another chemist described how the more careful of the horsemen used to make up the mixtures themselves, coming to him for only one or two of the ingredients and then passing on to another chemist, and perhaps even a third, to get the remainder.

Most of the information available today on the subject of horses and horse-whispering comes from the collection of books on country-lore that George Ewart Evans wrote during the 1960s. *The Pattern Under the Plough* and *The Horse in the Furrow* contain a treasure-trove of horse-lore from East Anglia, and much of what is in the public domain today has been taken from these two books, even if the extracts have not been credited! Also bear in mind that information given in modern books, which claim to give the genuine 'Word' can only have come from an oath-breaker – so it is doubtful whether these claims can be taken as authentic.

On this subject, perhaps it is wise to let George Ewart Evans have the last word, since he make a very valid point about many of the secrets of horse-lore:

The farm it has been said, is the last resort of magic. This is probably true; but we can now see that we must not interpret this word magic too uncritically. For it is part of magic's function to conceal its real dynamic under a smoke-screen of fustian and fantasy, precisely because magic is no longer magic if it ceases to be the monopoly of the class or section who practice it. A secret that is shared by the whole community has no realisable value, and brings no kudos – of status or actual economic advantage. Apart from the necessity of keeping their secrets for their own advantage, the old horsemen probably realised, however dimly, that it was to the society's advantage that their knowledge should remain esoteric. For in irresponsible hands the real secrets of the Word were dangerous ... where it was openly talked about, the self-styled practitioner boasted he had the word merely to gain status among his kind. In most instances what he had was the husk and not the kernel.

## Warning

**Always beware of those who claim this old knowledge for themselves and charge an exorbitant fee for treatment. The skills of the horse-whisperer cannot be bought, only bestowed – although a 'gift' would be expected to reflect the owner's circumstances and gratitude.**

## Horsehair Binding Spell

Horsehair taken from a horse's mane or tail is extremely strong and an important ingredient in binding spells. Here are two effective methods:

> ➤ Thread a needle with a single strand of horsehair, and then thread a number of acorns to create a 'rosary'. Each acorn should represent different aspects of the person (or persons) to be affected by the binding, and accompanied by a suitable spell or chant. If the spell is to bind lovers, it can be given to them as a gift; they then have the choice to break it at a later date, should they so desire. If more subtle results are required, the 'rosary' should be prepared in the normal way and then concealed in a lightening-blasted oak.

or

> ➤ Plait nine strands of horsehair and use it to bind a troublesome enemy. Prepare a poppet, or parchment image, and wrap tightly with the plait before placing in a sealed container or bottle. If your difficulties are on-going, keep the container close to hand (but not inside the house); if you wish to be completely rid of your enemy, throw the

container out with the rubbish, or drop it in a slurry pit.

## Points to ponder:

➤ Thought needs to go into whether the binding is to be carried out for selfish (revenge) or unselfish (protective) reasons.

➤ Binding the wrong person, or for the wrong reasons, can be counter-productive.

➤ Do you wish to leave yourself room to negate the spell in the future, should you wish to do so?

## Equine Correspondences: (Hunters and Runners)

**Arkle** is described as the greatest steeplechaser who has ever lived. He won three Cheltenham Gold Cups and was a phenomenally accurate jumper, who never fell on the racecourse. After sustaining an injury in 1966, he retired to the Duchess of Westminster's farm in Co. Kildare until his death in 1970. **Symbol: Greatness**

**Desert Orchid:** Possibly the most charismatic of steeplechasers whose fan club ultimately took over the horse and prevented his owner and trainer from running him in the Grand National. **Symbol: Popular favourite**

**Foxhunter:** Part of the famous show jumping duo with Harry Llewellyn who won a Gold Medal at the 1952 Olympic Games. A memorial was erected to Foxhunter on the Blorenge Hills overlooking Abergavenny, and when Sir Harry died in 1999, his ashes were scattered near the spot where his beloved horse was buried. **Symbol: Partnership**

**Golden Miller** was the focus of more drama and controversy in the 1930s than any other horse before or since. He won five Cheltenham Gold Cups, one in the same year as he won the Grand National. **Symbol: Legend**

**Gloria Victus** was a promising young steeplechaser who died before his time. Symbol: **Sacrificed to ambition**

**Man O' War:** The famous American racehorse who won twenty of his twenty-two starts, who retired early to stud and died in his thirst-first year. **Symbol: Fighting spirit.**

**Nijinsky** had a brilliant partnership with Lester Piggott, but ill-health put paid to his racing career and he retired to stud where his stallion fee was $300,000. **Symbol: Magnificence**

**Phar Lap:** The great Australian racehorse who began life as an 'ugly duckling' and grew into an international star. He died from poisoning in 1932 under mysterious circumstances. **Symbol: Tragedy**

**Phrenicos:** The horse of Hiero, of Syracuse, that won the Olympic prize for single horses in the 73 Olympiad. Its name means 'intelligent'. **Symbol: First and foremost.**

**Red Rum's** story is the stuff of fantasy fiction. From his uncertain beginnings he went on to win three Grand Nationals. Following his death in 1995 he was buried in the shadow of the winning post at Aintree. **Symbol: Against all odds**

**Shergar:** The gutsy little racehorse kidnapped and killed by the IRA. **Symbol: Martyrdom**

**Warrior:** Despite many near misses and with an uncanny gift for dodging bullets, Warrior was one of the last horses to serve Britain in war. After taking part in the great London Victory March, he returned to his birthplace on the Isle of Wight where he hunted, won a point-to-point and lived out a long retirement. **Symbol: Endurance**

# Chapter Five

# A Working Partnership

*There's to the horseman everywhere*
*Who keeps the secret at his heart*
*And who is always ready to take*
*A brother's part.*
The Quest for the Original Horse Whisperers, Russell Lyon

According to the entry in *Chinese Zodiac Signs:*

> Man has never truly conquered the horse, even if he has understood his language: underneath his apparent submission lies an unfathomable secret. Although he shares with man the most intense and violent adventures – even risking his life – he never gives of himself completely, as though some part of his most intimate self remains inaccessible and sealed from man, who aspires to enslave him.

On a much more practical and down-to-earth level, champion jump-jockey John Francome has observed:

> From the time that I used to walk my first pony up two scaffold planks into the back of my father's transit van to take him hunting, to the time when I had a thoroughbred yearling who would simply lie down whenever it didn't want to do something, horses have never ceased to amaze and amuse me. They can surprise you with their intelligence within moment of being unbelievably stupid, and astonish you with their strength as well as with their gentleness. To really understand them is something few people, including me, are able to do ...

A horse can produce all sorts of reactions in people. In *The Life, History and Magic of the Horse*, Donald Braider quotes Byron to emphasise the often confusing relationship between *'rider and horse, - friend and foe'* as two antagonists joined in their efforts.

> If it sometimes seems contradictory, it is because man was not always certain where he stood in relation to his indispensable ally, the horse, to which he at times ascribed supernatural powers and which, at others, he scorned and maltreated.

When the horse was at the height of its power, it was celebrated in art forms such as the Bayeux Tapestry, which shows the important role played by mounted soldiers during the Norman conquest of Britain. 'During subsequent centuries of war, the horse played a part second only to that of man himself.' So vital was the animal in the decisive outcome of a battle that almost every cavalry manual from every culture and time contains the direction to 'Kill the horse!' and the number of important battles in which the cavalry charge proved to be the decisive element are too numerous to count.

As history moved on, the lines that separated the 'war horse' from the 'pack horse' remain blurred. It is possible that the two-wheeled chariot was the first horse-drawn vehicle, but during peacetime, did the chariot become the cart to ferry around the wealthy? After all, horses were the rich man's prize and even the most wealthy would have been hard-pressed to keep a stable full of war-horses during times when men were not trying to kill each other.

Up to the 18th century, the use of the horse in civilian life was restricted to the monied classes of town and country, or to those who had to ride because of their employment. In the next stage of evolution, Donald Braider observes: 'Even in retrospect, not much glamour attaches to the horse and wagon, perhaps because there was not much glamour in daily life for the average human either. Whether the object drawn was a plough or a carriage, the work seemed drudgery for all concerned.'

Nevertheless, despite the initial belief that the horses' days were numbered, the age-old partnership of man and horse continues, even though its role as a major means of transportation had long passed into history. Machinery, however, cannot eradicate man's love affair with the horse. Horse-ownership is on the increase, as more and more people take up pleasure riding in its various form of racing, hunting, polo, dressage and eventing. Despite the gloomy predictions, the horse's place in society remains assured as equine events and establishments flourish.

Whether non-horsey people like to believe it or not, horses do get into the blood. It was only in recent years that an old farmer and horseman of my acquaintance lost the last of his faithful work-horses due to old age. For a long time he had shunned the use of mechanical equipment and preferred to attend to the yearly ploughing using a team of horses and it wasn't until age rendered them unfit for the heavy work that the farmer bought a tractor. Both animals lived out their retirement on the farm and were finally buried on the land they'd worked all their lives. 'Farm weren't the same after the last old 'orse had gone,' he said. 'Them two years were the most depressing I'd known and nothing seemed to prosper. In the finish I went down to the mart and paid £25 for a pair of scruffy old ponies, just to have about the place. From then on, the farm picked up and things felt 'right' again. Just having 'orses back on the land made all the difference.'

Another deeply entrenched facet of the horse tradition in the British Isles stems from the first horse-races held at Chester in the 1500s; the 'turf' remaining an exclusively British sport until the 19th century. The venue for medieval racing was the local fair: a periodic gathering that mingled business and pleasure, and at Smithfield's market in the late 12th century, trials were held between horses being offered for sale. Around 1540, at the Roodeye Fair, held on the banks of the Dee outside Chester, a silver bell valued at 3/6d was offered as a prize in a riding event at the direction of the mayor and the corporation. To quote from *The Illustrated Encyclopaedia of World Horse Racing*, 'A milestone had been reached: England was starting down a road which eventually led to it presenting the recognisable sport of horse racing to the world.'

Despite racing's humble beginnings at a local fair, Henry VIII took an interest and stabled his valuable horses at Greenwich and at the Royal Stud at Eltham. Elizabeth I founded a new stud at Tutbury and actively supported racing; and by the time of her death in 1601 events were also taking place at Carlisle, Richmond and Boroughbridge. As a result of his regular hunting trips across Newmarket Heath, James I established a royal stable there and his son and successor, Charles I, also favoured Newmarket for racing. It was Charles II, however, whose name will always be linked with the development of Newmarket as a racing centre.

The 17<sup>th</sup> century saw the beginning of the development of the famous race venues such as Doncaster, Lincoln and Epsom and around 1750, the Jockey Club was founded to lend some sort of leadership and authority to the sport. By 1800 there were 83 tracks and 536 registered horses in training.

It was in the year of Victoria's coronation that a humble Liverpool publican took the first steps towards the creation of a sporting event that would capture the imagination of the world in the years to come. Horse racing had taken place in the area since Elizabethan times, but these were tests of speed over a distance of flat, uninterrupted ground; when William Lynn leased the acreage at Aintree, he had intended to promote more of the same.

The first meeting took place in 1829 but Lynn decided to experiment with hurdle racing and by 1835 he was setting aside a fixture exclusively for hurdling. To quote Reg Green in *The*

*History of the Grand National*, 'The idea got off to a flying start when the most celebrated cross-country rider of the day (Martin Becher) arrived to take part.' Towards the end of 1838 a syndicate was formed and the plans went ahead for the 'Grand Liverpool Steeplechase' to be run in 1839 – later to become the Grand National.

Although it is constantly referred to as 'the sport of kings', horseracing draws a lot of support from people of all walks of life. Horses do get into the blood – even if you don't own one!

In some racing circles it is said that to change a horse's name is to change its luck – for good or ill. Not surprisingly, there are dozens of superstitions connected with horse racing, although most of them are personal. Some jockeys will put on the right boot first – start right, be right all day. Others dress in a certain order, leave the dressing room last, pull an ear, or wear certain 'lucky' underpants until they are in shreds – then wearing them under another pair!

Among one of the most well-known of jockeys' superstitions is the one that says new 'colours' must be broken in by throwing them on the floor and stamping on them. The logic behind this is that if a jockey wears new colours without this procedure, the rider is sure to get 'buried' at a fence or hurdle. According to jockey Willie Carson (who also owned a lucky blue suit), the new colours are now already dirty and there's no reason to fall off and get them dirty the hard way.

As we can see, the multi-billion pound industry of horseracing sprung from the humble horse fairs that were held periodically all over the country, dating back to medieval times. Up to the end of the 19th century they flourished all over Britain. Many of them have long since disappeared, but many Horse Fair Greens and Fair Field addresses remain in market towns to testify to the origins of such events. Those few horse fairs remaining are our last links with the great equine past and the atmosphere generated at such gatherings is reminiscent of the rowdy events where hard-working rural people allowed themselves to let their hair down for a while.

The horse fair at Stow-on-the-Wold in Gloucestershire is a relic of those times. In 1476 Edward II granted the Abbot of Evesham a royal charter to allow the town to hold a fair in May and October. With the dissolution of the monasteries, the charter fell to the lord of the manor, but the event continued as both an employment and animal fair. As the wool trade declined, horse-trading took over until the event became a horse fair. Stow, and a similar event at Appleby-in-Westmorland in Cumbria (which dates from 1685), are two of the few remaining horse fairs still running in England.

The Great Appleby Horse Fair is held in June and sees the town invaded by hundreds of farmers and gypsy horse-dealers. In Wales, up until recently, there was one held on Barley Saturday (last Saturday in April) at Cardigan, Dyfed. Its programme opened with a grand parade of stallions of many traditional breeds, from shire horses to highly bred hunters, which were led through the town. During the 1990s, the gypsies who formed the nucleus of the Stow-on-the-Wold event were pushed out of the town square and, aware that the fair was becoming marginalised, decided to preserve this 'vibrant element of English rural history'. Four families bought the fair field and despite an injunction from the district council preventing them from parking up for the event, the current mayor is a passionate supporter. 'We *should* celebrate the fair as a part of Stow's rural history and be grateful to the gypsies that it continues,' is her opinion.

But even with a renewed interest in modern horsemanship, the horses' link with the supernatural remains, especially in rural areas. As most experienced riders can recall, there are those certain places on lonely roads and track-ways where the horse refuses to pass. An acquaintance tells of the October afternoon when she and her mount were caught out by an unexpected rainstorm …

Dark storm clouds were gathering and a few spots of rain had started to fall. A wide grass verge ran along the quiet road, which was bordered by tall trees, with fields on either side and the odd farm set back off the road. We were going in the direction of home and the pony was pulling hard, certainly more than happy to keep up a cracking pace. At the time I remember feeling a bit jittery about the storm but I was more anxious to get back to the yard.

Within about twenty yards of the road's end, the pony suddenly shied violently and began rearing in the road. After a considerable battle I had him standing still and tried urging him forward. Again he reared and I had an awful job preventing him from bolting back the way we'd come. To go back would have added another hour and a half to the journey and it was almost dark. By now the heavens had opened and the rain was lashing down. As a last resort I took off my jacket to put over his eyes, leading him around in tight circles. After a few moments of this, I sensed a shift in his manner and went for it; throwing myself back in the saddle just in time as the pony bolted, but at least he was galloping in the direction of home this time.

Anyone could be forgiven for thinking that the storm had played a major part in this affair – except for another incident in exactly the same place a few years later, told by the same lady, but about a different horse and rider.

About four years later, my husband was late in coming back from a ride. Some inner instinct told me something was wrong, so I set off to walk in the direction I knew they would take. I hadn't gone far when I saw them approaching up the track, and it was obvious things had gone badly wrong. The horse was lame and distressed, and bleeding from a cut knee; while my husband was slumped in the saddle, his face chalk-white with blood trickling down from under his cap.

It seems that the ride had been going fine until they got within a few yards of the end of the road where my own mount had shied. Being young and strong my husband's horse had gone into a spectacular fit of the vapours and unseated him, despite him being a very experienced horseman. He was never clear about what happened after that. He remembered picking himself up and limping after the horse, who by this time was standing on the grass verge some way back up the road, shaking like a leaf. A passing motorist had stopped and taken hold of the bridle but there was little else she could do in those pre-mobile phone days. The horse shied again at the same spot and rather than risk a fatal accident to either of them, my husband was forced to return by the longer route.

Were these instances down to chance? Some fifteen years earlier a horrific murder had taken place at that spot: an elderly lady had been dragged from the road into the fields, where she was repeatedly raped and stabbed. A man walking his dog had found her badly mutilated body the following morning; and the murderer turned out to be a local man from a nearby village.

That was all forty years ago now, but to this day I do not like the energies at that spot. Is it some silent fear in the air, generated by the murder victim from all those years ago? Or is it the spirit of the place? Talking to friends who still live locally, they all agree that the place gives them the creeps even though it remains unspoiled countryside; the fields are green and the trees magnificent. The murder has been forgotten as the old people of the village have moved away or passed on. The new-comers to the place probably know nothing about it, but yet something almost evil still remains there – and I do not use the word lightly.

It would be easy to pass off my experiences as simply being a case of me transmitting my apprehension of the darkness and approaching storm to the pony ... but as to my husband's accident? A grown man and an experienced and capable horseman to boot; on a glorious spring morning, riding his own familiar horse? Could the place itself have inspired the murder?

It was certainly a strange case as the murderer was a local man, married with two children and no previous criminal record. His victim was a popular, unassuming lady who worked in the village sweet shop; she was elderly and certainly not dressed to attract the attention of a sex attacker. The murder took place at 5.30 one winter's evening. Her rape had been brutal and repeated beyond belief, even continuing long after she was dead. Her body had been dragged over a total of four fields, indicating that this was a frenzied but sustained attack.

Could this be an instance of Horned God energy going wrong? Or being over-amplified in some way? Is this a hot-spot for the true Wild Hunt? And is this what the horses picked up on? Certainly something terrified them beyond reasoning at exactly the same spot and to this day, in spite of this being a 'horsey' area, I have never known any horses to be grazed in those adjoining fields.

Horses have always been associated with 'unquiet spirits'. Faerie horses and horsemen are an integral part of British folklore; they could travel from place to place at fantastic speeds, once they had used the magical chant: *Horse and Hattock!* and using ragwort seeds for a steed. This is probably yet another Victorian addition to Faerie-lore, since ragwort is deadly to horses (and other livestock), it would be highly unlikely that *anyone* having any equine empathy would put the plant anywhere near the animals, even symbolically!

Many tales are told of the 'Faerie Rade', when they were encountered riding in procession, on white horses hung with silver bells. The story of the last 'Faerie Rade' comes from Scotland and was told by the writer Hugh Miller more than 100 years ago. A herd-boy saw them and asked of the last rider to pass him, who they were and where they were going. 'Not of the race of Adam,' replied the rider, 'The People of Peace shall never more be seen in Scotland.'

Witches and the Faere Folk, often inseparable in folk-belief, were blamed for tangling the manes of horses and riding them undetected in the night. As a magical defence against such mischief, an amulet in the form of a 'hag-stone', a stone with a hole in it, was hung inside the stable door. In many stables where horses are still kept, you will often find a 'hag-stone' hanging from the rafters over the stall, or by the door. This is a piece of stone or flint with a natural hole bored through it and suspended by a piece of string or wire. This amulet has various names in different areas of Britain: a holy-stone, a ring-stone or a hag-stone. Attaching iron to the stone gives it added potency since this repels negative influences.

Aubrey wrote in his *Miscellanies*: 'To hinder the Night Mare they hang on a String a Flint with a hole in it (naturally) by the Manger; but best of all, they say, hung about their necks … It is to prevent the Night Mare *viz*. The Hag from riding the Horses who will sometimes sweat at Night. The Flint thus hung does hinder it.' And from Herrick's *Hesperides*:

*Hang up hooks and sheers to scare*
*Hence the hag that rides the mare,*
*Till they be all over wet*
*With the mire and the sweat.*
*This observed, the manes shall be*
*Of your horses all knot free.*

Here we have superstition clouding what is, in fact, a very old witch belief. The use of the hag-stone has been hijacked from being a witch's defence against negative forces, to a repellent against witches themselves. This is a common occurrence in fairly recent folklore collections and must rank alongside trying to repel a Jewish vampire with a crucifix!

It's also a common belief that both witches and the Faere Folk were said to take horses from the stable for a midnight ride and return them the next morning lathered and sweating – although colic would probably have been the correct diagnosis in the majority of cases. Witches and the Faere-Folk also knew that *sacred* iron repelled negative or evil influences, but as the centuries passed the lore became perverted, and by the 16th century the belief remained that witches and the Faere Folk could be repelled by the use of iron horseshoes and hag-stones. The term 'hag' was often used in earlier times as a substitute for Faerie, and the Faere-Folk were supposed to teach their supernatural skills to witches.

Throughout this book, we have seen how old traditional British folklore, particularly that surrounding horses, has been twisted and perverted to mean the exact *opposite* to that which our ancestors believed. Hag-stones, iron, horseshoes and nails, which were used magically in the past to avert negativity, are now seen as charms used for repelling witches, the Faere Folk and evil!

## The Hag-Stone Charm

Hag-stones are small stones or flints that have had holes bored in them *naturally*. The smooth pebbles found on the seashore are often the work of a tiny marine creature that bores its way into the stone, leaving the wear of the waves to complete the job. Those found inland are usually pieces of rough flint that have worn into the most amazing shapes and in this instance the hole is usually worn through by weathering.

The protective elements of a hag-stone can be called upon to protect a home and its occupants from negative energies. Should you be fortunate enough to discover one for yourself, or if you receive one as a gift from a friend, do not attempt to cleanse it. What you should do is a thorough magical cleansing of your home and once this is completed, the hag-stone should be placed by the front door, suspended by a cord – or preferably nailed through with iron! In the stable, the hag-stone should be hung from a beam nearly over the centre of the horse's head or back, about eighteen inches above head height. Or it should be nailed above the stable door.

## Warning

- A manufactured hag-stone does *not* have the same magical properties as those created naturally.
- Many shops sell commercially produced stones, so beware of fakes.
- A stone that has been polished will have had the natural protective properties removed
- Do not remove a hag-stone that has been placed there by another witch, no matter how tempting.
- Giving away a hag-stone is to give away luck, so these should only be presented to someone special.
- Do not cleanse a hag-stone as they are a purely protective charm and do not carry negative energies.

## The Hag-Stone Stable Curse

This is an interesting protective curse, which was used in a racing yard when it was discovered that someone was interfering with the riders' tack. One work rider was always assigned an extremely dangerous horse as the first ride out of the morning and it was discovered before leaving the yard (and crossing a busy main road) that both buckles had been undone on the bridle and carefully looped back, so that the pin did not go through the leather. Any pressure on the bridle and the reins would have come away in the rider's hands.

This action was tantamount to severing the breaks on a car, as the horse was a known rogue and needed all the rider's skills to keep it steady. Had it played up when crossing the road, there could have been a dual fatality. Unfortunately, there was no way of knowing for sure who the perpetrator was and so the following curse was thrown in the tack room:

*Let the hands that do the mischief,*
*be the hands that take the fall*

Suspicion had fallen on one particular person who had left another yard after a similar incident, but from that day the rider kept a hag-stone in their bag, and silently repeated the curse each time they entered the tack room, whilst holding the hag-stone. Eventually, the person who had been suspected took a nasty fall on the gallops and was injured so badly that they could not continue working in racing.

Whether the malicious actions of the perpetrator were meant as a joke is immaterial, sooner or later there would have been a serious, if not fatal, accident. Making the curse general, rather than aiming it at an individual, safeguarded the *sender* from targeting the wrong person.

## Herbal

Both of these plants can be used symbolically in magic to denote 'horse power'.

**Horse-chestnut:** If a slip is cut close to a joint, it will present a perfect miniature of a horse's hock and foot, show and nails.

**Horse-vetch:** This plant has pods shaped like a horseshoe and is sometimes called the 'horse-shoe vetch'.

## Equine Correspondences (Working)

**Black Bess:** The famous mare ridden by the highwayman, Dick Turpin, which, tradition says carried him from London to York in record-breaking time. **Symbol: Speed and strength.**

**Black Saladin:** The Earl of Warwick's famous charger, which was coal black. Its sire was Malech and, according to tradition, when the race of Malech failed, the race of Warwick would fail. And it was so. **Symbol: Destiny.**

**Bucentaur:** The city of Venice still pays tribute to the horse that bore the Crusaders where no Venetian vessel could pass. **Symbol: Against all odds**

**Copenhagen:** Wellington's charger at Waterloo. It died in 1835 at the age of twenty-seven. **Symbol: Steadfastness**

**Marengo:** Napoleon's favourite white charger that was captured after the Battle of Waterloo. Its remains are now in the Museum of the United Services, London. It is represented in Vernet's picture of *Napoleon Crossing the Alps*. **Symbol: Imperialism**

The horses of Mary, Queen of Scots: **Black Agnes**, the palfrey of Mary, Queen of Scots, given by her brother Moray, and named after Agnes of Dunbar, a countess in her own right and **Rosabell**, her favourite palfrey. **Symbol: Frippery**

**Molly:** Sir Charles Napier's mare who died at the age of 35. **Symbol: Constant**

**Roan Barbary:** The favourite horse of Richard *II* '*When Bolingbroke roade on Roan Barbary/That horse that thou so often did bestrid.*'(Shakespeare; *Richard II* ) **Symbol: Change of fortune.**

**Ronald:** Lord Cardigan's thoroughbred chestnut, with white stockings on the near hind and fore feet. It carried him through the Balaclava charge. **Symbol: Courage under fire.**

**Rossignol:** The palfrey of Madame Chatelet of Cirey, the lady with whom Voltaire resided for ten years. **Symbol: Companionship.**

**Savoy:** The favourite black horse of Charles VIII of France; so called from the Duke of Savoy who gave it to him. It had but one eye and was 'mean in stature'. **Symbol: Hidden beauty**

**Sorrel:** The horse of William III, which stumbled by catching his foot in a mole heap. This accident ultimately caused the king's death. Sorrel like Savoy was blind in one eye and 'mean of stature'. **Symbol: Things left to chance.**

**Suleiman:** The favourite charger of the Earl of Essex. **Symbol: Glamouring.**

**White Surrey:** The favourite horse of King Richard III. *'Saddle White Surrey for the field tomorrow.'* (Shakespeare: *Richard III* ) **Symbol: Resignation.**

Chapter Six

# Magical Lore

*Humans would inevitably see horses through their own eyes,*
*their dreams and ambitions, myths and fears,*
*vanities and fashions.*
The Nature of Horses, Stephen Budiansky

To fully understand the magical dynamics of equine energy, it is important that we neither trivialise nor sentimentalise the power behind it, and an extract from the Dick Francis novel, *Straight*, seemed to bring us full circle to where we came in at Chapter One. Here the hero (himself a jump-jockey like the author), reflects on the inner driving force that determines the character of a particular winning horse he rides:

> The will to win was born and bred in them all, but some cared more than others: it was those with the implacable impulse to lead a wild herd who fought hardest and oftenest won. Sports writers tended to call it courage but it went deeper than that, right down into the gene pool, into instinct, into the primordial soup on the same evolutionary level as the belligerence so easily aroused in homo sapiens, that was the tap root of war. I was no stranger to the thought that I sought battle on the turf because, though the instinct to fight and conquer ran strong, I was adverse to guns. Sublimation, the pundits would no doubt call it. Datepalm and I both, on the same primitive plane, wanted to win.

For our distant ancestors the cosmic turbulence visible from the Earth could easily have been visualised as the thundering of horses' hooves, the flashes of lightening the sparks that flew from the celestial shoes and chariot wheels. According to *Man, Myth & Magic*, mythology makes much of the famous 'Wind Horses', such as Pegasus and Hofvarpnir, (the steed of Gna, messenger of Frigg) accompanying these violent storms were the terrifying winds and driving rain, often seen as great armies joined in battle beyond the black clouds obscuring them from view. And out of this aerial violence came the legend of the Wild Huntsman, 'with his thundering horse and baying hounds, searching the highways and byways for luckless souls, who happened to get in his way'.

A real horse that surely symbolises this ancient 'hell on earth' is what has been described as one of the greatest thoroughbreds of history: Warrior – who belonged to General Jack Seely. Over four million horses died in the Great War but Warrior not only survived but was trained to stand still under machine gun fire. To cap it all he returned to win a point-to-point, eventually being put down in his thirties and buried on the Isle of Wight. Warrior is certainly up there with Wellington's more famous Copenhagen, and Seely, so legend has it, even recommended Warrior for a VC. By comparison, Copenhagen was unceremoniously dismantled after death, and his hooves mounted and presented to various cavalry regiments.

The power, speed and pride encapsulated in the horse is not one with which we can easily assimilate, even on a shamanic level, for the reasons that Dick Francis again observes in *Whip Hand*:

Beautiful, marvellous creatures whose responses and instincts worked on a plane as different from humans' as water and oil, not mingling even where they touched. Insight into their senses and consciousness had been like an opening door, a foreign language glimpsed and half learned, full comprehension maddeningly balked by not having the right sort of hearing or sense of smell, not sufficient skill in telepathy. The feeling of oneness with horses I'd sometimes had in the heat of a race had been their gift to an inferior being; and maybe my passion for winning had been my gift to them.

If we wish to utilise and tap into this elusive and primordial strength as a focus for magical working, it *must* be with a high degree of trepidation and a *lot* of respect. This is not energy that we can control or negotiate with; if we log-on then we must be prepared to be trampled and kicked in return. It also reflects the fact that people either know or fear horses – there is no middle ground and this is how it should be with their magical energies. Our 'knowing' gives us the understanding to interact with equine energy, but there should be no disgrace in fear either. Like all magical pathways, equine-energy is not for everyone and the wisdom is in the knowing: and understanding when to walk away.

Despite the primordial influence the horse still has over mankind, as George Ewart Evans points out, the richest combination of surviving beliefs and customs centred in the heavy horse up to the first part of the 20$^{th}$ century when horses were still an important part of British farming. So here we have those two different types of energy: the war-horse (which includes the hunters and racers) and the workhorse. The differences may be subtle but they are there, and they are important!

## Divination

The ancient form of divination from horses is known as *hippomancy*, where not only the behaviour and colour of horses were taken into account, but also the pattern of their hoof prints, and even the amount of dust created by their movements. It is thought that *hippomancy* originated at the time of the European Celts, who had sacred horses that walked in procession behind a chariot while the seers divined the future from the animals' movements. As the Celts moved into the British Isles, they brought their divinatory methods with them. Folklore tells us that they kept white horses in sacred groves, training them to walk only in a certain area; after the horses passed by, diviners interpreted the prints left in the dirt.

The early Germanic tribes also kept special horses in their temples where seers foretold the future by observing the manner in which divine horses emerged from the sacred enclosure – right foot forward indicated a favourable outcome, while the left foot called for a recount. If a warlord was planning to conquer another tribe, a negative reading meant that the war would be delayed until a more favourable time.

Observing animal behaviour, otherwise known as *alectry-omancy*, is also another ancient form of divination although in modern times the appearance of a certain coloured horse, for example, is viewed as lucky or unlucky, rather than a form of prediction. Willie Carson tells the story of fellow-jockey Harry Carr who once spotted a skewbald pony in a field while on his way to the races. When this happened, Harry had to get hold of his right toe with his left hand and hold it until he saw another four-legged animal. "That's not so outrageous, you might say. No, except that Harry was driving his car at 70 mph when the skewbald appeared, and refused to stop and let anyone else drive!'

Many of us inherit these minor divinatory superstitions as something we've grown up with, although a horse may be lucky or unlucky, depending on the different parts of the country (or world) from which our families originate. For example, many British believe that a black horse is lucky, and a piebald is unlucky, while in Europe the reverse is true. English country folk are very uneasy about white horses, while the most ominous sight for Americans to come across is a red-headed girl on a white horse.

## The Conjuration of Orobas

The ultimate in equine divination, however, and certainly not for the foolish or faint-hearted is the conjuration of the daemonic form of Orobas, who can be found in such journals as *The Goetia* by Aleister Crowley; *The Book of Black Magic and of Pacts* by Arthur E. Waite; *Dictionary of Demons* by Fred Gettings; *The Discoverie of Witchcraft* by Reginald Scott and *Dictionaire Infernal* by Collin de Plancy.

Orobas is known as the fifty-fifth Spirit of Solomon and a 'Great Prince' who appears as a horse but when commanded will assume human form. He will give any answers about the past, present and future, including 'good dignities and advancements, with the favour of friends and foes; he gives true answers of Divinity, and of the Creation of the World'. Unlike many other daemons, Orobas is a protective spirit and remains faithful to the magician, defending him from the attentions of negative forces. He is consulted because he is prepared to give an accurate response to questions concerning the future and to reveal untruths.

To invoke him, take a copy of his Seal and write the question for which you require an answer on the reverse side. Place a white candle (or night light) inside the crescent of a *cast* horseshoe and use this as the focus for summoning your magical energies. Either allow the answer to come through in the form of a pre-arranged symbol, or use the pendulum.

**Warning:** Beware of the information you seek: the truth often hurts!

## Pathworking to The Wild Hunt

No book on equine magical lore would be complete without some *practical* reference to the Wild Hunt with its legion of ghostly horses and baying hounds. Ideally, this should be worked between All Hallows and Winter Solstice, on a day of high winds and storm clouds – and must be performed out of doors since the

Wild Hunt has no part in 'lounge-craft', there being more than an element of risk in the undertaking.

It is commonly believed in folklore that to see the Wild Hunt as it sweeps by is extremely dangerous. If a person is unable to find shelter, they are advised to lay face downwards on the ground, or shelter in the lee of a large tree until the dark company has passed. To deliberately look at the riders, or to speak to them, is to invite death, madness, or a dreadful personal misfortune. Anyone who attempts to outrun the Wild Hunt may be seized and carried away, or killed as a result of the encounter.

Out in open countryside on a stormy day, it is possible to summon up the Wild Hunt if the magician keeps his wits about him. Stand in an exposed place, near a stand of mature trees and, facing into the wind, take a deep breath, drawing the cold wind into your lungs. As the dark storm clouds sweep by overhead, visualise the figures of riders, with their horses and hounds in the changing shapes; hear the music of the hounds in the howling of the wind.

Should you feel the mounting tension that gives the impression you are being pursued by some powerful unstoppable force, resist the urge to run; take shelter in the lee of a large tree and sit on the ground. If you have a dog with you, make sure that you keep a firm hold of its collar, as it may be seduced into joining the pack. Allow your mind to travel free and link with the wild natural activity that is going on all around you; draw on the strength and power that is generated by the company and project it into whatever magical channel you feel is appropriate.

**Warning: This pathworking is included for interest purposes only and should not be attempted by inexperienced practitioners due to the often unexpected and highly dangerous results that can occur on both the psychic and physical level.**

## Equine Correspondences (Romantic)

**Alfana:** Gradasso's horse in *Orlando Furioso.* The name means 'a mare'. Gradasso, was King of Sericana and was the 'bravest of all the pagan knights who went against Charlmagne with 100,000 vassals in his train'. **Symbol: Loyalty**

**Aquiline:** Raymond's steed bred on the banks of the Tagus in Tasso's *Jerusalem Delivered.* The name means 'like an eagle'. Raymond was the Master of 4,000 infantry and Count of Toulouse, equal to Godfrey in the 'wisdom of cool debate'. **Symbol: To soar**

**Bajardo:** Rinaldo's horse, of a bright bay colour, was once the property of Amadis of Gaul. It was found by Malagigi, the wizard, in a cave guarded by a dragon, which the wizard slew. According to tradition it is still alive, but flees at the approach of man, so that no one can hope to catch him. The word means 'bay coloured'. *Orlando Furioso.* **Symbol: Elusiveness.**

**Cerus:** The horse of Adrastos, which was swifter than the wind. The name means 'fit'. Andrastos was an Indian price from the banks of the Ganges, who aided the King of Egypt against the Crusaders. He wore a serpent's skin and was slain by Rinaldo. (Tasso: *Jerusalem Delivered* ). **Symbol: Fitness**

**Bayard:** FitzJames's horse from Sir Walter Scott's epic tale, *Lady of the Lake.* **Symbol: Obedience.**

*Stand, Bayard, stand! The steed obeyed*
*With arching neck, and bended head,*
*And glaring eye, and quivering ear,*
*As if he loved his lord to hear.*

**Bevis:** The horse of Lord Marmion, from Sir Walter Scott. The word is Norse and means 'swift'. **Symbol: Swiftness.**

**Bayardo:** The famous steed of Rinaldo, which once belonged to Amadia of Gaul. Bayardo's Leap is the name given to three stones, about thirty yards apart, near Sleaford. It is said that

Rinaldo was riding Bayardo when the demon of the place sprang up behind him. The horse, in terror, took three tremendous leaps and unhorsed the fiend. **Symbol: Coping with the unexpected**

**Brigadore** (or Brigliadore) Sir Guyon's horse, which had a distinguishing black spot in its mouth, like a horse shoe in shape. From Spencer's *Faerie Queen*. **Symbol: Hidden qualities.**

**Brigliadoro**: Orlando's famous charger, second only to Bajardo in swiftness and wonderful powers. The word means 'golden bridle'. *Orlando Furioso*. **Symbol: Rarity**

**Brontes:** One of the horses of the Sun or a blacksmith's art personified – the name signifies 'thunder'. **Symbol: Secret arts.**

*Not with such weight, to frame the forky brand,*
*The ponderous hammer falls from Brontes' hand*
[Hoole: *Jerusalem Delivered*, book xx]

**Bronzomarte:** The horse of Sir Launcelot Greaves; the word means 'mettlesome sorrel'. **Symbol: Mettle**

**Capilet:** The grey horse of Sir Andrew Aguecheek (Shakespeare: *Twelfth Night*). A capilet, or capulet is a small wen on a horse's hock. **Symbol: Small imperfection**

**Comrade:** Fortunio's fairy horse. **Symbol: Gift of the Faere Folk**

**Curtal:** The bay horse of Lord Lafeu (Shakespeare: *All's Well That Ends Well.*) The word means 'cropped'. **Symbol: Cut away**

**Cut:** The carrier's horse (Shakespeare: *Henry IV* ). A familiar name of a horse – the word may be taken to mean either 'castrated' or 'cropped'. **Symbol: Gelded**

**Ferrant d'Espagne:** The horse of Oliver. The name means 'the Spanish traveller'. **Symbol: Traveller**

**Fiddle-back:** Oliver Goldsmith's unfortunate pony. **Symbol: Unprepossessing**

**Frontaletto:** Sacripant's charger - the name means 'little head'. (Ariosto: *Orlando Furioso*). **Symbol: Slow witted**

**Granē:** Seigfried's horse, of marvellous swiftness. The name means 'grey-coloured'. **Symbol: Speed**

**Grizzle:** Dr Syntax's horse, all skin and bone. The word means 'grey coloured'. **Symbol: Hidden charm**

**Hirondelle:** The ageing mare belonging to *Julie de Carneilhan's* brother, which he took with him when he left Paris for good. 'He, at least, is taking with him what he loves best in the world' (Colette) **Symbol: That which is prized above all others.**

**Jenny Geddes:** Robert Burn's mare. **Symbol: Poetic burden**

**Marocco:** Bank's famous horse. Its shoes were of silver, and one of its exploits was to mount the steeple of St Paul's. **Symbol: Amazing**

**Passe Brewell:** Sir Tristram's charger (*History of Prince Arthur*). **Symbol: Companion**

**Rabicano:** Argalia's horse in *Orlando Innamorato*, and Astolpho's horse in *Orlando*. **Symbol: Popular**

**Furioso:** Its dam was Fire, its sire Wind; it fed on unearthly food. The word means a horse with a 'dark tail but with some white hairs'. **Symbol: Elemental.**

**Rosinante:** Don Quixote's horse, all skin and bone. The word means 'formerly a hack'. **Symbol: Trustworthy.**

**Shadowfax:** The untameable 'prince of horses' from Tolkien's *Lord of the Rings*, who carries Gandalf into battle. **Symbol: Salvation**

**Vegliantino:** The famous steed of Orlando, called in French romance *Veillantif*, Orlando being called Roland. The word means 'the little vigilant one'. **Symbol: Vigilance.**

## Chapter Seven

# The Celestial Horse

Year Of The Horse: 1906 : 1918 : 1930 : 1942 : 1954 : 1966 : 1978

It must now seem strange that with all this affinity with the horse, in both history and legend, that apart from Sagittarius there isn't a real equine representation in the Western Zodiac. There are, however, equine constellations:

> **Equuleus**, or 'the Little Horse', which is said to represent Celeris, brother of Pegasus, given to Castor by Mercury and featured in Bayer's *Uranometria* (1603);

> **Monoceros**, the Unicorn, portrayed in the constellation cards, *Urania's Mirror* (1825);

> **Pegasus**, the Winged Horse, illustrated by Domenico Bandini in his 15th century encyclopaedia of the universe, *Fons Memorabilium Univers*.

For more celestial imagery of 'horse power', it is necessary to travel to the other side of the world — and consult the Chinese astrologers. According to legend, the Buddha invited all the animals in creation to help him celebrate the New Year. Only twelve animals responded, and they arrived in the following order: the Rat, Ox, Tiger, Rabbit, Dragon, Snake, Horse, Goat, Monkey, Rooster, Dog and Pig (some traditions replace the Rabbit with the Cat and the Pig with the Wild Boar).

To thank them, the Buddha offered each one a year that would be dedicated to him alone through the ages. This year would carry the animal's name, and express his symbolic character, which would be passed on to those born during that year. This established a twelve-year cycle to coincide with the order in which the animals arrived at the New Year celebrations – the horse representing the seventh month.

In truth, Chinese astrology predates the influences of Buddhism by about 1,000 years and developed in almost total isolation from the systems of India, Babylon, Egypt and Greece. Not only is each year symbolised by an animal, it also corresponds to one of the five elements (water, fire, metal, wood and earth). This means that among those borne as a Horse (sociable, energetic, strong-willed, opinionated and sporty), one might be a Water-Horse, another might be a Metal-Horse and a third an Earth-Horse, etc., so that the Horse characteristics are correspondingly modified by the appropriate element – with the whole cycle taking 60 years to complete.

The other characteristics of those born in the 'Year of the Horse' are loyalty and enthusiasm, tempered with a strain of unpredictability, a tendency to flare up easily and impatience. He (or she) will be enterprising and ambitious, but with a fear of being fenced in. Being herd animals, the people of the horse require support and encouragement and hate silence and any lack of communication.

The horse is a chthonic creature, mythically emerging from the bowels of the earth or the depths of the sea; but it is also the symbol of the spirit of the corn and the seeds of regeneration. In Chinese astrology, there is a further complication in that every 60 years is the year of the Fire Horse (1906 and 1966 were Fire Horse years; the next will be 2026). Under the normal rules of astrological prediction the years ending in the number six are dominated by the water element.

'This regular replacement of Water by Fire, insofar as the Horse is concerned, is one of the mysteries of Chinese astrology, and we must forego all rational argument when considering it,' says *Chinese Zodiac Signs*. Needless to say, to be born during the Year of the Fire Horse has both its advantages and disadvantages:

since both the qualities and the defects of the Horse will be multiplied by ten!

It would be a simple mistake to think that Chinese and Western astrology were synonymous with each other, but although the two systems are distinct, they are never contradictory. Unlike Western astrology, however, each of the Chinese signs is a 'small universe' in itself, with its own laws and dominions and completely independent of all other signs.

## The Four Seasons of the Horse

**This superficial overview of Western astrological signs linked to those born in the Year of the Horse (see page 85) is included purely for interest.**

## For Those Born in Spring
### Horse/Aries

This is a sprinter rather than a long-distance runner, although with a capable hand on the reins s/he might excel themselves. A good-natured individual who is happier being led rather than as a leader. Capable of great devotion, the Horse/Aries can be managed with only a small degree of subtle psychology.

### Horse/Taurus

This *is* a long distance runner, but can also carry a grudge for a long period of time, too. If held back, the Horse/Taurus will seethe inwardly and although his/her anger is rarely expressed, it can be devastating when unleashed. S/he can be creative and sentimental, generous but often intolerant with a low boredom threshold.

### Horse/Gemini

Predominantly a 'show-horse' who likes to be around people who appreciate the entertainment value. Self-assured and easily adaptable, s/he often runs the risk of not being taken seriously.

Can be slightly irresponsible and lacks a certain amount of discipline in carrying out jobs s/he doesn't find rewarding, or 'showy' enough.

## For Those Born in Summer
## Horse/Cancer

Comfort and security are essential ingredients to keep the Horse/Cancer happy. 'At a well-managed stud farm he will be unequalled in performance; running wild in nature he will become fearful and bitter.' His/her private life is more important than anything else and if s/he has a secure base, there is nothing s/he can't achieve

## Horse/Leo

This is the Arkle or Red Rum of the champion stakes and s/he loves every minute of the thrill of the chase and the roar of the crowd. Proud and headstrong, s/he has to be active; pawing the ground and rearing if his jockey holds him/her back. The Horse/Leo is a record breaker and will clear every obstacle in his/her path.

## Horse/Virgo

A well-balanced and reliable mount, the Horse/Virgo will achieve a respectable success in his/her undertakings. S/he is resourceful and practical; the flamboyant spectacular of the parade ring is not for him/her. His/her routine follows a strict discipline and his/her sense of duty is a remarkable asset on a professional level.

## For Those Born in Autumn
## Horse/Libra

An elegant dressage horse, with a luxurious coat and mane, who cannot bear the idea of 'a hair out of place'. Nevertheless, s/he is adaptable and socially agreeable — although there is an underlying thought that s/he will never love anyone as much as s/he loves themselves. The Horse/Libra appreciates the power of speech and is a passionate debater on subjects close to his/her heart.

## Horse/Scorpio

The horse with a red ribbon on its tail, since it will lash out with both barrels if someone comes up too close behind. Fiercely independent, impassioned and revengeful, Horse/Scorpio demands that anyone close to him/her must respect his/her independence and liberty. Life with him/her could be likened to a rodeo circus, so be prepared to hang on for grim death.

## Horse/Sagittarius

This is one of the great 'hunters and runners', the horse that goes out for the sheer enjoyment of the chase, rather than to emerge as the winner. Providing the Horse/Sagittarius has a purpose or goal, s/he will achieve it; otherwise they will amble along with a total disregard for those who rely on them. Generous, with a strong sense of honour.

## For Those Born in Winter
## Horse/Capricorn

'This noble and honest Horse is the most virtuous, persevering and courageous of them all.' S/he does not swerve from the path once it has been set but often more personal relationships can suffer as a result because of her/her sense of obligation to a career or other commitment. The Horse/Capricorn will persevere to the end even when the odds are against him/her.

## Horse/Aquarius

Intuitive and unstable, the Horse/Aquarian always has an eye on the future, often without paying sufficient attention to the here and now. It is often difficult to pin him/her down to a definite opinion, but if s/he is not personally involved there will be no end to the help and advice s/he is willing to give.

## Horse/Pisces

Romantic and liking security, the Horse/Pisces nevertheless is completely at ease within the world of illusion and often attempts to swim with currents over which s/he has no control. Very susceptible to the influence of others, s/he on the other hand, can be extremely opportunistic if the right circumstances allow. Always seeking new truths and new perspectives.

## The Horse and the Five Elements

Whereas in Western occultism and astrology the elements (earth, air, fire, water and sometimes spirit) are linked to planetary and zodiacal symbols, in Chinese astrology, each year is joined to an element: water, fire, wood, metal and earth. It also follows that each of the twelve 'emblematic' animals is linked successively to each of the five elements.

These are the primary, elemental forces affecting the universe and it is their particular association with each sign that provides the basis for every horoscope and the continuance of the life-cycle. Wood gives birth to fire, which gives birth to earth, which gives birth to metal, which gives birth to water, which gives birth to wood.

In order to calibrate the element corresponding to each year of birth, see below:

Years whose digits end in:
2 and 3: Water
6 and 7: Fire
4 and 5: Wood
0 and 1: Metal
8 and 9: Earth

For Horse-people, Chinese astrology has an uncommon knack of being embarrassingly accurate, simply because the mystical importance of the animal has been acknowledge for thousands of years. And even if you weren't born in any Year of the Horse, there may still be some revelations for all Rats, Oxen, Tigers, Rabbits (or Cats), Dragons, Snakes, Goats, Monkeys, Roosters, Dogs and Pigs (including Wild Boars)!

In tribal cultures, in which both the shaman and the witch have their distant roots, the power animal is an individual's 'other self', a creature to which that person's life is inextricably bound by common ancestry. And it is therefore important to honour our 'power horse' as such. In modern cultures we are not taught to value animals, or to acknowledge the gifts they bring into our life – and the world around us. On a personal level by honouring our 'power horse' we acknowledge that otherworldly binding; that the spirit of the animal is giving up its 'freedom' in order to enhance our spiritual development. This can be as simple as saying a silent 'thank you'; or acquiring an object that represents our 'power horse' and putting it where we can see it as we go about our daily tasks. By honouring our 'power horse' we make a deeper connection with it on both spiritual and temporal levels that will last a lifetime ... and those lifetimes to come.

Moon Books invites you to begin or deepen your encounter with Paganism, in all its rich, creative, flourishing forms.